World Freemasonry

World Freemasonry

An Illustrated History

John Hamill
and R. A. Gilbert

Aquarian/Thorsons
An Imprint of HarperCollinsPublishers

Frontispiece
Freemasons' Hall, London, headquarters of the United Grand Lodge of England. Built 1927-33 as a memorial to those brethren who were killed in the Great War 1914-18. Architects H.V. Ashley and Winton Newman.

The Aquarian Press
An Imprint of HarperCollins*Publishers*
77-85 Fulham Palace Road,
Hammersmith, London W6 8JB

Published by The Aquarian Press 1991

1   3   5   7   9   10   8   6   4   2

A CIP catalogue record for this book is available from the British Library

ISBN 1 85030 722 8

Typeset by Harper Phototypesetters Limited,
Northampton, England
Printed in Hong Kong by
HarperCollinsManufacturing

Contents

Acknowledgements

UNLESS otherwise stated the illustrations are from the collections of the United Grand Lodge of England. The authors are grateful to the Board of General Purposes of the United Grand Lodge of England for permission to reproduce the illustrations. They are also grateful to David Peabody who produced the photographs.

Introduction

TO ATTEMPT a detailed world history of Freemasonry in one small volume is an impossibility. Over a hundred years ago the great Masonic scholar R. F. Gould attempted it in three large volumes. Since his day not only has Freemasonry greatly expanded throughout the world but our knowledge of its history and development has greatly increased. What we have attempted to do in this book is to give a factual account of Freemasonry's rise, development, and expansion throughout the free world. The result is something of an aperitif which we hope will lead some, at least, to feast on the wealth of detailed material available to those who wish to study a particular aspect of an institution that has attracted men from all stations and walks of life for over 300 years.

Men of rank and of great eminence in many fields of human endeavour have involved themselves in Freemasonry, but its great and enduring strength has been the countless number of ordinary men who have both enjoyed the fellowship they found in Freemasonry and have found their religious beliefs and moral principles strengthened by the lessons they have learned in lodge. Reasons for joining and remaining in membership are many and diverse but all are founded in a common belief that Freemasonry, based on the principles of Brotherly Love, Relief, and Truth, can only be a force for good in society. In our materialistic age any organization promoting morality and principle seems to be regarded as highfalutin and strange. Nevertheless, Freemasonry has stuck to its initial impulse and continues to try to turn good men into better citizens, working for the common good and not individual advancement.

It is a sad comment on the present state of society that an organization promoting such ideas is immediately suspect and open to attack. It cannot, and has not, been denied that a very few Masons have been rotten, spectacularly so in some cases. It would be incredible if among the millions of men who have been and are Freemasons there had not been a few rotten apples. Freemasons are as human as any other group of men. Examination of the facts, rather than relying on hearsay and folklore, shows that those who have erred would have done so regardless of what organizations they belonged to and that Freemasonry played no part in their wrongdoing.

That said, this book is in no way an apology for Freemasonry. We have simply, and in as comprehensible a way as possible, attempted to give an overview of strands within a very complex and complicated subject. Much has been written both for and against Freemasonry. We have tried to be as neutral and dispassionate as we can, dealing in verifiable facts and making it clear where we are dealing with theories or opinions. Where opinions are given they are our own. Fellow Freemasons may regret that we have included material on anti-Masonry. For that we make no apology. To have omitted any reference would have given an incomplete picture and resulted in accusations of partiality or white-wash.

Freemasonry a secret society and world wide conspiracy? Anyone reading this, or any other sane book on the subject, will find that neither statement is true. Criticism from ignorance is easy. Had half the writers attacking Freemasonry had the honesty to go to source and ask questions they would have found, as we hope this book shows, that their questions would have been honestly answered. It is a strange secret society that raises no objections when its members not only speak but also write about it.

January 1991

J. M. HAMILL
R. A. GILBERT

1
Origins and Early Development

OR OVER a hundred years Masonic historians have been arguing over the origins of Freemasonry. Their arguments have been hampered by two major problems. First, there is the paucity of primary evidence necessary to prove any one theory. Second, there is the mass of material, written by both Masonic and non-Masonic writers, which appears to prove conclusively a particular theory. Masonic historiography has been bedevilled by well-meaning writers who have glossed over gaps in evidence, misinterpreted evidence, invented evidence, accepted obvious forgeries as evidence, and taken similarities between Freemasonry and other organizations as meaning that they either linked up with each other, had a common ancestor, or grew out of each other.

The general consensus amongst Masonic historians today is that Freemasonry originated within the British Isles and that it descends directly or indirectly from the operative stonemasons who built the great cathedrals and castles of the Middle Ages (Figs. 1-2). Because so little evidence has survived, or has not yet been discovered, no one can state categorically which of those two theories is correct. Of the two, the theory of a direct descent from operative Masonry would appear to have the most evidence to support it, but there are difficulties in linking the evidence together and differences of interpretation of some of that evidence.

The theory of a direct descent from operative Masonry states that there were lodges of stonemasons which were units controlling the mason's trade. In the 1600s these lodges began to accept men who were not stonemasons, calling them accepted Masons. Gradually these accepted Masons became the majority in the operative lodges and transformed

them into speculative lodges. Thus you had three stages: operative lodges; transitional lodges; and speculative lodges.

On the face of it the surviving evidence would appear to prove this theory. Two great scholars, Knoop and Jones, spent many years studying the surviving archives of the great medieval buildings in England and established that the operative Masons were grouped in lodges to protect and control their trade. In Scotland the Schaw Statutes of 1598-9 show that operative lodges in Scotland were becoming geographically defined units. From 1599 onwards there are surviving minute books of Scottish operative lodges which imply that some form of ritual work was going on in addition to the management of the mason trade. In London from the 1620s the London Mason's Company appears to have had an inner circle, the Acception, whose membership was a mixture of members of the company and accepted Masons with no connection with the company or operative masonry. In the seventeenth century the Scottish operative lodge minute books increasingly show the admission of accepted Masons. Some of these operative lodges still exist today and their records show that by the early eighteenth century they had lost their

1 **Left**
Operative Masons at work. A carved panel on the frieze of the church of San Michele, Florence.

2 **Far left**
The Crypt of York Minster. Engraving used by the York Grand Lodge, c.1780, to show their links with York and operative Masonry.

3 **Left**
Sir Christopher Wren (1632-1723). Engraving by J. Smith after a portrait by Kneller.

operative functions and had become lodges of Freemasons.

To all appearances we have a direct link, but appearances can be deceptive and a close examination of the evidence and the addition of evidence of other contemporary events throw up a number of anomalies. The first problem is that there is no evidence of operative lodges in England after about 1500 and certainly no evidence of operative lodges accepting non-operatives. The second problem is that in England in 1646 Elias Ashmole was made a Free Mason in a lodge specifically called for that purpose. Ashmole records the names of all those present and none of them had any operative connections. Nor is there any evidence that the lodge was a permanent one, simply a group of Freemasons forming a temporary lodge for a specific purpose. Other English evidence from the seventeenth century points to similar circumstances: the lack of operative lodges and the making of Freemasons by other Freemasons with no operative connections. Indeed Randle Holme III makes a specific differentiation between the operative Company of Masons and the Society of Freemasons.

The keystone of the direct link theory is the existence of Scottish operative lodges admitting non-operatives; but how much value can we place on this as evidence of speculative Freemasonry? We do not know what form of ritual was worked in those lodges. We do not know if the ritual was altered for the admission of accepted Masons. Because of this

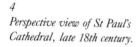

4
Perspective view of St Paul's Cathedral, late 18th century.

5

King George VI MS of the Old Charges, 1727, with the Arms of the London Masons Company. One of 110 versions, dating from 1390, still extant.

lack of evidence we do not know what effect, if any, the accepted Masons had on the operative lodges. On the basis of our present evidence we believe that the accepted Masons in Scottish lodges were simply honorary members, not the first speculative Freemasons. Their position appears to have been similar to members of the Royal Family in England today who are inducted into many groups and societies, of which they have no practical experience, as honorary members of patrons.

Those who support the direct descent theory dismiss the lack of evidence for standing operative lodges in England by claiming that the evidence must have been destroyed and that because of the closeness of England and Scotland what happened in Scotland must also have happened in England. This is to ignore the totally separate historical, political, religious, legal, and social developments in Scotland and England. Until the union of the two crowns in the person of James VI of Scotland and I of England, Scotland and England were totally separate and distinct nations. Indeed for much of the 1400s and 1500s Scotland had closer ties and more in common with France than it had with its southern neighbour.

It is because of these two conflicting strands—the existence of Freemasons without operative connections and the lack of operative lodges in England, combined with the existence of operative lodges in Scotland admitting accepted Masons but no evidence for Freemasonry without operative connections—that, on the basis of our present evidence, we find we cannot accept the theory of a direct descent.

Those who support the indirect link theory have approached the subject from a slightly different viewpoint. In addition to looking for evidence for early Freemasonry they have addressed the question of *why* Freemasonry should have developed. The principal figure in the development of the indirect link theory was the late Brother Colin Dyer who, in a paper to Quatuor Coronati Lodge, examined the differences between the oldest and the third oldest version of the manuscript *Old Charges*, the Regius MS of *c.*1390, and the Grand Lodge No. 1 MS of 1583. The Regius MS definitely has a purely operative content; on the other hand, the Grand Lodge MS contains much that has no relevance to operative Masonry but a great deal of relevance to Freemasonry. He then looked at the basic idea behind Freemasonry and the period in which the later versions of the *Old Charges* began to appear (Fig. 5).

The period in which these altered versions of the *Old Charges* began to appear, and in which supporters of the indirect link theory believe that Freemasonry originated, the late sixteenth and early seventeenth centuries, was one of great intolerance in matters of politics and religion in England. Men of differing views of religion and politics were unable to meet in harmony. Indeed so divisive were those subjects that families and friendships were broken because of different views, and eventually England was torn by bloody civil war.

As far as can be established the ban on the discussion of religion and politics has always existed in Freemasonry. Similarly Brotherly Love, or, as we might express it today, tolerance, has always been one of the three great principles forming the foundation of Freemasonry. Thus those who formulated the theory of an indirect link between operative and speculative Masonry believe that those who established Freemasonry were men of peace who wished to bring an end to religious and political strife. To achieve this they founded a brotherhood in which politics and religion had no part and dedicated themselves to a belief in God and the three great principles of Brotherly Love, Relief and Truth. In practical terms they wished to form a society that would enable men of differing views to meet in harmony and to work for the betterment of mankind.

In the period in which they were working, the late sixteenth and early seventeenth centuries, the method of teaching and passing on philosophical ideas was by means of allegory and symbolism. As the central message of Freemasonry was the building of a better man in a better world what better way to arrange the society than to take over the form of the old operative lodges and to use the working tools of the operative craft as symbols upon which to moralize (Fig. 6)? To match the central message, what better allegory than an actual building? Despite high levels of illiteracy the one book with which the great majority of the population was intimately familiar was the Bible, a central source of allegory. The only building described in any detail in the Bible is King Solomon's Temple, of which there are slightly conflicting detailed descriptions in the Book of Kings and the Book of Chronicles. Additionally, the idea of King Solomon's Temple as a cosmic symbol had long fascinated artists and philosophers (Fig. 7).

In an intolerant world any attempt to promote toleration would have to be done quickly to avoid the suspicion that those of differing views were not meeting together for subversive reasons. By clothing themselves in the guise of a philosophical and charitable organization which also indulged in conviviality, so the indirect theory runs, the originators of Freemasonry hoped to achieve by means of example their aim of promoting tolerance.

The initiation of Elias Ashmole (Fig. 8) in 1646 is significant in the indirect link theory. It should be remembered that it took place at the height of the English Civil War. Ashmole was a Royalist who had been captured by the Parliamentarians and was on parole at the house of his father-in-law, a leading supporter of the Parliamentarians in the north-west of England. Those who formed the lodge to initiate Ashmole were a mixed group of Royalists and Parliamentarians.

The theory of an indirect link is very new and needs more research for

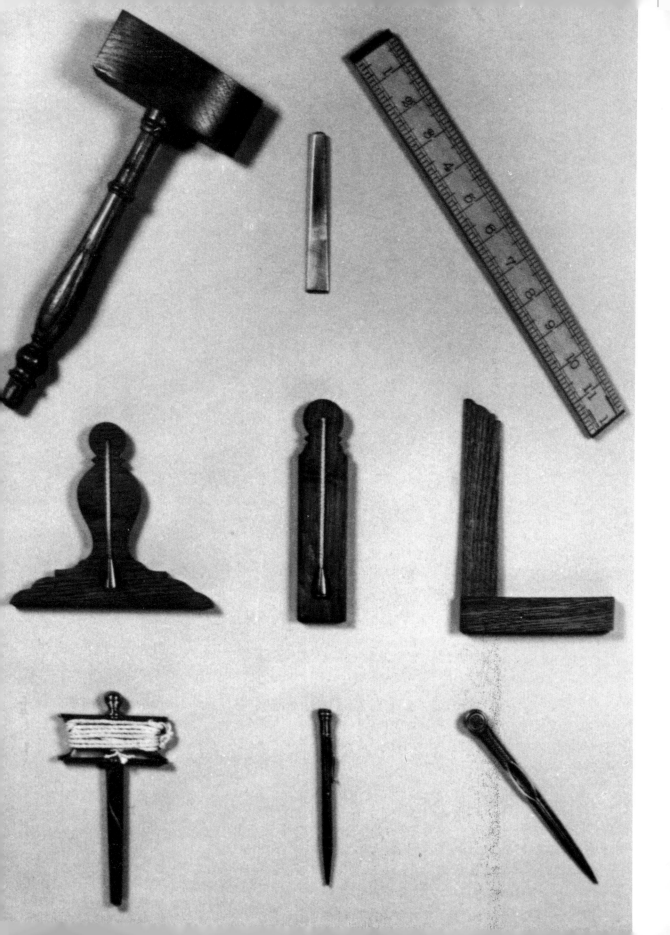

it to carry as much weight as the theory of a direct link with operative Masonry. Despite its highly speculative nature, the theory of an indirect link is important because it is the first to ask not *how* and *where* Freemasonry originated, but *why*. In all the work that has been done to try and prove the direct link theory no one has asked why the non-operatives wished to become accepted Masons and why they turned a trade orientated organization into a speculative art.

English Freemasons never doubted that their craft had descended—albeit by a tortuous and probably untraceable route—from the operative lodges of medieval stonemasons; nor did it concern them that men from all walks of life met together for the work of the Lodge. Their 'peculiar system of morality'—and its attendant ceremonies—were accepted as being open to almost every stratum of society: however undemocratic English society as a whole might be, within the lodge all men were treated as equals.

Such an egalitarian attitude did not spread to the continent of Europe. In France—still an absolute monarchy with virtually no democratic institutions—Freemasonry was effectively the preserve of the nobility and of the professional classes, who viewed it variously as either an extension

6 Left
The working tools of an operative Mason, used by Freemasons to symbolize the moral rules they are to follow.

7 Below
A 17th century engraver's impression of King Solomon's Temple. In post Renaissance times the Temple was depicted as an enormous palazzo or Gothic pile.

of their other social activities, or as a path to esoteric knowledge. For their purposes the three Craft Degrees, with their unassuming ceremonies and straightforward moral message, were too simple and too dull. For those with such a viewpoint, to justify their membership of the Craft it had to be shown to have a more elevated purpose and a more illustrious origin than could be found in a mere reconstructed building guild. In 1737, to their great satisfaction, such a purpose and such an origin were provided.

On 21 March 1737, Andrew Michael Ramsay, a Scottish Jacobite, convert to Roman Catholicism, and Chevalier of the Order of St Lazarus (awarded to him by the Duc d'Orleans), delivered a speech to the Grand Lodge in Paris in his capacity as official Orator. His Discourse—or 'Oration' as it is more commonly known—was the only certain act of Ramsay's otherwise obscure Masonic career; but in the history of the Craft as a whole it was an event of immense significance.

Much of Ramsay's speech was unexceptionable: 'We desire', he said, 'to reunite all men of enlightened minds, gentle manners, and agreeable wit, not only by a love for the fine arts, but much more by the grand principles of virtue, science and religion, where the interests of the Fraternity shall become those of the whole human race.' He continued in similar vein: 'The second requisite of our Society is sound morals', to which end 'Our festivals are not what the profane world and the ignorant vulgar imagine. All the vices of heart and soul are banished there, and irreligion, libertinage, incredulity, and debauch are proscribed' and 'in order to prevent [such] abuses . . . women are excluded from our Order'. The ends of brotherly love and charity were also stressed, and that the Craft has secrets in the form of 'figurative signs and sacred words' was admitted, as was 'the taste for useful sciences and the liberal arts'. But above and beyond all this, Ramsay emphasized the origins of the Craft.

The word Freemason must therefore not be taken in a literal, gross, and material sense, as if our founders had been simple workers in stone, or merely curious geniuses who wished to perfect the arts. They were not only skilful architects, desirous of consecrating their talents and goods to the construction of material temples; but also to religious and warrior princes who designed to enlighten, edify, and protect the living Temples of the Most High.

More specifically:

At the time of the Crusades in Palestine many princes, lords and citizens associated themselves, and vowed to restore the Temple of the Christians in the Holy Land, and to employ themselves in bringing back their architecture to its first institution. They agreed upon several ancient signs and symbolic words drawn from the well of religion in order to recognize themselves amongst the heathen and Saracens. These signs and words were only communicated to those who promised solemnly, and even sometimes at the foot of the altar, never to reveal them.

8 **Opposite**
Elias Ashmole. A contemporary portrait copied for Grand Lodge from the original in the Ashmolean Museum.

9

St John's Gate, Clerkenwell. 18th century engraving. A Hospitaller fortress that is now home to the Venerable Order of St John.

10

Medieval Templars, now used as a seal on certificates by the (Masonic) Great Priory of England.

Freemasonry was thus 'an order founded in remote antiquity, and renewed in the Holy Land by our ancestors' who also 'formed an intimate union with the Knights of St John of Jerusalem. From that time our Lodges took the name of Lodges of St John (Fig. 9). Thus union was made after the example set by the Israelites when they erected the second Temple, who whilst they handled the trowel and mortar with one hand, in the other held the sword and buckler'. After this, 'the kings, princes and lords returned from Palestine to their own lands, and there established divers Lodges'.

Ramsay went on to draw connections between lodges in France and in Scotland; to give a fanciful account of the Order's preservation in England; and to conclude by stating that 'From the British Isles the Royal Art is now repassing into France'—much to the delight of his French audience. In all, Ramsay had created an amazing, imaginative and historically most improbable and unsupported pedigree for the Craft: and yet it was a pedigree that struck a responsive chord.

The idea of Freemasonry descending from medieval chivalric orders immediately caught the continental imagination. Ramsay's 'Oration' was printed in 1741 (in the *Almanach des Cocus*; an earlier printing in 1739 in *Lettres de M.V.* was not widely noticed) and within a decade a host of new rites and degrees ('Additional' to the Craft Degrees), based on the ideals of chivalry and on contemporary notions of knightly practice, had sprung up in France and Germany. Many of these were putative 'Templar' degrees, for although Ramsay had made no reference to the Knights Templar—and it should also be noted that the Knights of St John of Jerusalem (the Hospitallers) were bitterly hostile to the Templars—the notion of a Masonic descent from the Templars became firmly embedded in the romantic mind of continental Masonry (Fig. 10). Ramsay himself founded no additional degrees whatsoever, but his Oration undoubtedly inspired their creators: 'For the next 100 years after 1740 the compilation of rituals of new degrees went merrily on, multiplying beyond belief'. Many of these degrees, as we shall see, claimed an origin for themselves within Templarism or its analogues.

But was there any historical basis for the claim of a Templar origin for Freemasonry? To answer such a question one must first look at the true nature of the Knights Templar. The Order of the Poor Knights of the Temple of Solomon had been founded in 1118 by Hugh de Payens, a Burgundian knight who, with seven of his companions, took a solemn oath to protect pilgrims *en route* to the holy places in Jerusalem. They undertook also to observe the religious virtues of poverty, chastity, and obedience, and in 1127 obtained for the Order a formal Rule—based on that of the Cistercians—from St Bernard of Clairvaux. Initially, they took as their headquarters a part of the site of Solomon's Temple, but as the military/religious order expanded many other religious houses (known as preceptories) were set up both in Palestine and throughout much of western Europe.

The Templars were unquestionably professed members of a religious order, but there were certain noticeable points of distinction between them and other, non-military orders: the hierarchy of the Order of the Temple was based on a military command structure; the Order was responsible directly and only to the Pope; and professions to the Order were made not openly but in secret, so that the ceremony of initiation was a matter of conjecture for non-members. There is no question as to the dedication of the Templars to their professed aims, or of their bravery; but eventually the Holy Land was lost to Islam and the original *raison d'être* of the Order disappeared. However, the integrity of the Templars, the security of their preceptories, and their possession of an independent naval fleet, had led to their developing an equally important role as bankers and financiers throughout Christian Europe. The wealth that this brought them inevitably excited the avarice of temporal rulers, and in 1307 Philip the Fair of France instigated the process that would lead to their destruction.

Acting on the basis of charges of blasphemy, heresy, immorality, murder, and treachery—charges which were almost certainly trumped up—Philip

JACQUES DE MOLAI.
Dernier Grand Maître
des Templiers
Brulé à Paris, le 19 Mars 1513.

11
Jacques de Molay, last Grand
Master of the Knights Templar.

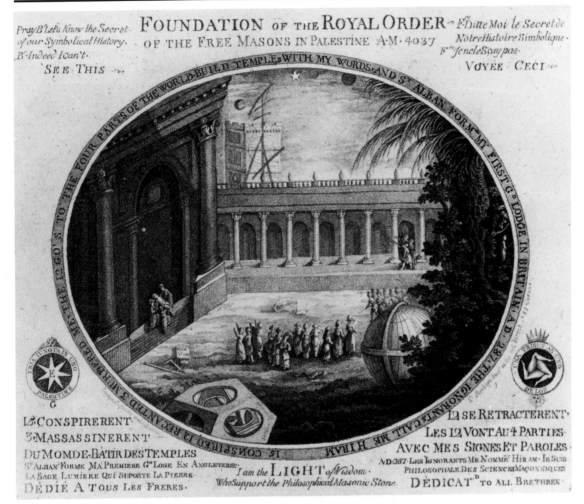

12
Symbolic engraving by Peter Lambert de Lintot, c.1770, linking Solomon's Temple, the Knights Templars and Rosicrucianism to the origins of Freemasonry.

ordered the arrest of all the Templars within his domains. Notwithstanding the lurid confessions (following on barbaric torture), the Pope, Clement V, protested and a halt to the process was called. But the Pope was weak and a creature of Philip's. In 1308 a Papal Bull ordered the arrest of Templars throughout Europe (those in Scotland evaded arrest, thus begetting legends of secret Templar survivals); a papal commission investigated the charges against them, and after a long and involved process the Order was finally suppressed in 1312, the Templar estates passing to the Knights Hospitallers. Two years later the Grand Master of the Templars, Jacques de Molay (Fig. 11), and his principal officers were burned at the stake, protesting their innocence to the last. And with their deaths the Order of the Temple passed from history into legend.

On the surface there is nothing whatsoever to connect the Templars with the Masonic order that arose 400 years later, but from the middle of the seventeenth century onwards historical works on the Templars had begun to appear both in England and on the continent. The most important of these (Dupuy's *Traitex . . . scavoir la Condemnation des Templiers*, 1654) was admittedly extremely hostile, but it did bring the Templars to public notice, while in England they had been praised and defended by George Buc (in 1631) and by Elias Ashmole (in 1672). Ashmole, of course, was an 'accepted' Mason and so the fanciful connection between Templars and Freemasons was not a difficult one for the imaginative to make.

And there are certain parallels between the two Orders: the secrecy surrounding the admission of new members; the hierarchical structures; and the mutual concern with King Solomon's Temple. But nowhere in Freemasonry can one find injunctions to celibacy, poverty, and a monastic life; the Masonic legend is concerned with building the Temple, not with the quartering of one's horses within it; and there is not the slightest evidence that the Order of the Temple survived in any form even for four

13
Robert Fludd, an English Rosicrucian whose works were widely circulated in Europe.

decades, let alone for four centuries. There is, indeed, not the slightest
historical support for the Templar theory of origin. But no matter: for those
with a vision of chivalry, such difficulties were minor problems to be
glossed over. They wished Freemasonry to be derived from Templarism;
ergo, it *was* so. They could never have guessed where their fantasies would
ultimately lead.

In much the same way, other would-be Masonic historians—and
creators of grandiose rites—saw the Craft as a child of the Rosicrucian
movement. Unlike the dreams of the Templar enthusiasts, there might
seem at first sight to be some substance to this theory—if, that is, one can
prove that the Rosicrucians ever existed. The Knights Templar were an
historical reality, but no such certainty attaches to the Brethren of the Rosy
Cross. All that can be said is that in the early years of the seventeenth
century a curious work, the *Fama Fraternitatis*, which set out the nature,
history, and aims of the 'Laudable Fraternity of the Rosy Cross', was
circulating in Germany in manuscript form. In 1614 this first Manifesto
appeared in print, to be followed in the next two years by the *Confessio
Fraternitatis* and the *Chymische Hochzeit* (Chemical Wedding). All three
works were subsequently translated into most of the major European
languages, and all three inspired the literati of Europe to rush into print
with commentaries either attacking or defending the manifestos, their
anonymous authors, and the putative Brotherhood.

But who—if they existed at all—*were* the Rosicrucians? Their history is
given in the *Fama*, but it is very much the stuff of legend. 'The Chief and
original of our Fraternity', declared the *Fama*, was one Christian
Rosencreutz, a German whose parents, though noble, were poor and
obliged to place their son in a monastery while he was still a child. In due
course, but while still a youth, he travelled to the Holy Land, visiting wise
men at Damascus ('Damcar') who had anticipated his coming and from
whom he learned both medicine and mathematics. After translating the
mysterious Book 'M' into Latin, the young Christian Rosencreutz travelled
first to Egypt and then to Fez in Morocco, where he continued his
studies—apparently in magic and the Hebrew Cabbala—for two years
before sailing for Spain and returning to his native Germany after further
wanderings in Europe.

Once safely home, Rosencreutz established the Fraternity of the Rosy
Cross with the aid of three of his former monastic brethren. They built
a home for themselves—The House of the Holy Spirit—brought in four
more brethren, 'all bachelors and of vowed virginity', and set about
perpetuating their Order. It had six basic rules:

1   That none of them should profess any other thing than to cure the sick, and that *gratis*.
2   None of the posterity should be constrained to wear one certain kind of habit, but
    therein to follow the custom of the country.

3   That every year upon the day C. they should meet together in the house *S. Spiritus*, or write the cause of his absence.

4   Every brother should look about for a worthy person, who, after his decease, might succeed him.

5   The word C.R. should be their seal, mark, and charter.

6   The Fraternity should remain secret one hundred years.

These six articles 'they bound themselves one to another to keep, and five of the brethren departed, only the brethren B. and D. remained with the father, Fra. R.C., a whole year; when these likewise departed'.

Each year they held their assembly and the Order prospered, but eventually all the original brethren died. Christian Rosencreutz himself lived to the age of 106 years and died in 1484, but all knowledge of the site of his tomb was lost until 1604, when it was rediscovered by chance. The door to the tomb bore the inscription 'Post 120 annos patebo' ('After 120 years I will open'), and on opening it the tomb proved to be a seven-sided vault, lit by an ever-burning lamp and with the perfectly preserved body of Christian Rosencreutz lying in an altar. On this altar was a brass plate inscribed variously with a series of mottos: *Jesus mihi omnia* ('Jesus, all things to me'); *Nequaquam vacuum* ('A vacuum exists nowhere'); *Legis Jugum* ('The Yoke of the Law'); *Libertas Evangelii* ('The Liberty of the Gospels'); *Dei Gloria Intacta* ('The Whole Glory of God'). Also within the vault were books and manuscripts concerning the secrets of the Order, and although the vault was duly sealed again, the author of the *Fama* promised that some of those secrets would be revealed to the world at large.

The brethren are all said to have followed the Reformed religion, but did not condemn other Christians (the *Confessio*, however, is violently anti-Roman while being more forthcoming than the *Fama* on the Order's philosophy). Indeed, the whole thrust of the Manifestos is to announce a new Reformation, a revelation of hitherto secret knowledge, and the imminent regeneration of mankind. It is worth quoting the opening paragraph of the *Fama* in full:

Seeing the only, wise and merciful God in these latter days hath poured out so richly his mercy and goodness to mankind, whereby we do attain more and more to the perfect knowledge of his Son Jesus Christ and Nature, that justly we may boast of the happy time, wherein there is not only discovered unto us the half part of the world, which was heretofore unknown and hidden, but he hath also made manifest unto us many wonderful, and never heretofore seen, works and creatures of Nature, and moreover hath raised men, imbued with great wisdom, who might partly renew and reduce all arts (in this our age spotted and imperfect) to perfection; so that finally man might thereby understand his own nobleness and worth, and why he is called Microcosmus, and how far his knowledge extendeth into Nature.

14 **Opposite**
Elias Ashmole. Engraved by Fairthorne c.1676. Ashmole was supposed to be the English proof of the Rosicrucian origins of Freemasonry.

The final Manifesto, the *Chemical Wedding*, is, in the words of Frances Yates, 'a romance about a husband and wife who dwell in a wondrous castle full of marvels and of images of Lions, but is at the same time an allegory of alchemical processes interpreted symbolically as an experience of the mystic marriage of the soul—an experience which is undergone by Christian Rosencreutz through the visions conveyed to him in the castle, through theatrical performances, through ceremonies of initiation into orders of chivalry, through the society of the court in the castle.' It is quite distinct from the other Manifestos. Its author is known to have been a Lutheran theologian, Johann Valentin Andreae, although it is far from certain that he also wrote the *Fama* and *Confessio*, and it does not convey their fervent message of moral regeneration.

But what was the effect of the Manifestos at the time of their publication? Responses to them were of three kinds: attacks, defences, and pleas from those who wished to join the Fraternity; but after an initial burst of enthusiasm the pamphlet writers died away, leaving the idea of the Rosicrucians to be incorporated in the broader stream of hermetic and alchemical thought, thence to be fished out as occasion demanded by such men as Thomas Vaughan or Elias Ashmole (Fig. 13).

It has been argued by Frances Yates that the influence of the Manifestos was a continuing one; that the ideals of tolerance, and of the sharing of knowledge that they urged, encouraged, if they did not actively inspire, the growth of such bodies as the Royal Society. This is a plausible theory, and it is also not inherently improbable that some aspects of Rosicrucian thought may have inspired those who created the first speculative Masonic lodges; but something rather more substantial than the notion of moral inspiration is needed if we are to advocate Rosicrucianism as a direct and significant source of Freemasonry.

The earliest suggestions of a Rosicrucian influence on Masonic origins (offered—needless to say—without any supporting evidence) come in the course of a number of humorous jibes against Freemasonry published in the 1720s. In 1730 a letter to the *Daily Journal* for 5 September argued that:

There is a Society abroad from whom the English Free-Masons (asham'd of their true Origin, as above) have copied a few Ceremonies and take great Pains to persuade the World that they are derived from them, and are the same with them. These are called *Rosicrucians*, from their Prime Officers being distinguished on their High Days with Red Crosses . . . On this Society, have our Moderns, as we have said, endeavour'd to graft themselves, tho' they know nothing of their most material Constitutions, and are acquainted only with some of their Signs of *Probation* and *Entrance* . . .

The first serious suggestions of a Rosicrucian origin did not come until 1782 with C. F. Nicolai's *Das Entstehen der Freymaurergesellschaft*, in which

15
French symbolic plate c.1740.
The simple symbolism of the
working tools belies any
Rosicrucian or Templar origins.

he argues that there really *were* Rosicrucians, and that all those present at Elias Ashmole's initiation into Freemasonry at Warrington in 1646 were members of the Rosicrucian Order. A more rational view was taken by J. G. Buhle who, in 1804, maintained that the Manifestos were part of a hoax but that Rosicrucians did, nonetheless, lie behind Freemasonry. Buhle's work is known in England through Thomas De Quincey's extremely free 'translation' as the *Historico-Critical Inquiry into the origin of the Rosicrucians and the Free-Masons*. He claimed, in De Quincey's words, that:

The original Free-Masons were a society that arose out of the Rosicrucian mania, certainly within the thirteen years from 1633 to 1646, and probably between 1633 and 1640. Their object was *magic* in the cabbalistic sense: *i.e.* the *occult wisdom* translated from the beginning of the world, and matured by Christ; to communicate this when they had it, to search for it when they had it not; and both under an oath of secrecy.

That this argument is a nonsense was clearly shown a century ago by A. E. Waite, who pointed out (in his *Real History of the Rosicrucians*, 1887, pp. 403-4) the essential differences between Freemasonry and Rosicrucianism. Freemasonry, said Waite,

has never been at any period of its history an association for scientific researches and the experimental investigation of Nature, which was a primary object with the Rosicrucian Brotherhood. It has not only never laid claim to the possession of any transcendental secrets of alchemy and magic, or to any skill in medicine, but has never manifested any interest in these or kindred subjects. Originally an association for the diffusion of natural morality, it is now simply a benefit society. The improvement of mankind and the encouragement of philanthropy were and are its ostensible objects, and these also were the dream of the Rosicrucian, but, on the other hand, it has never aimed at a reformation in the arts and sciences, for it was never at any period a learned society . . . It is free alike from the enthusiasm and the errors of the elder Order . . . it has been singularly devoid of prejudices and singularly unaffected by the crazes of the time. It has not committed itself to second Advent theories; it does not call the Pope Antichrist; it does not expect a universal cataclysm.

All of which points are telling ones, but esoteric writers on Freemasonry have lacked (and still lack) Waite's balance. More than one 'authority' who should have known better has maintained the Rosicrucian fiction. John Yarker, for example, stated that 'Sir Robert Moray and Elias Ashmole, who were received Masons in 1641 and 1646 respectively, were both of them diligent students of Occult matters, and it is within the bounds of probability that the Rosicrucians may have organized a system of the Craft degrees, upon which they superadded their own Harodim receptions long before Free-Masonry passed to the Grand Lodge in 1717' (*The Arcane Schools*, 1909, p.431).

This, however, is comparatively restrained when compared with the claims of that bane of critical Masonic historians, the Revd F. de C.

16
Anthony Sayer. Elected the first Grand Master of England, 24 June 1717. Victorian oil portrait from a contemporary engraving.

Castells. In one of his most wayward books, *Our Ancient Brethren the Originators of Freemasonry* (1932), Castells maintained that 'At length the historic Rosy Cross of the sixteenth-century Manifestos was diversified and gave rise to Freemasonry' (p.292) and argued further that 'the Rosy Cross had continued as an Invisible Society, and now in 1765 it reappears under the designation of the Royal Arch' (p.296). Such nonsense is in itself of no consequence and ought to be no more than a minor irritation to the historian; but it has had another and more unfortunate consequence in that it has provided ammunition for the motley and rabid crew of professional anti-Masons who seize upon every titbit of misinformation for their own dubious ends. For them, as for Masonic fantasists, the need to distinguish between fact and fancy in the question of Masonic origins has

17
Rev Dr J.T. Desaguliers, a Huguenot divine and physicist. Grand Master 1719. Reputed to have introduced the nobility and intelligentsia to Freemasonry.

18
1723 Constitution's frontispiece showing the Duke of Montagu (GM 1721) handing the Constitution to Philip, Duke of Wharton.

19 Far right
Col John Pitt wearing the regalia of a Grand Steward, which office he held in 1732.

never been recognized; but for the Masonic historian a more objective view is a prerequisite, and given such a view he must necessarily find both the Rosicrucian and Templar theories devoid of substance.

If we do not know how or when Freemasonry originated, we do know when *organized* Freemasonry began. On 24 June 1717 four London lodges came together at the Goose and Gridiron Ale House, St Paul's Churchyard and formed themselves into a Grand Lodge. They elected Anthony Sayer (Fig. 16), Gentleman, Grand Master and resolved to meet annually for a Grand Feast. Initially this appears to have been all that was intended. There was no suggestion that the Grand Lodge was to be a regulatory body or that its jurisdiction was to be more than the Cities of London and Westminster. By 1721, however, when John, Duke of Montagu (Fig. 18) became the first *noble* Grand Master, lodges outside London began to apply to come under the Grand Lodge's jurisdiction, quarterly meetings began to take place, and the Grand Lodge assumed a supervisory role. By 1730 it had taken charge of or constituted over a hundred lodges in England and Wales; had issued its first code of regulations, the 1723 *Constitutions*; appointed a Secretary to keep records of its meetings; appointed Provincial Grand Masters to superintend lodges and stimulate interest in the Provinces; set up a central charity fund; and begun to export Freemasonry abroad by issuing dispensations to constitute lodges in Spain and India.

The events in England had not gone unnoticed in Ireland. Evidence for early Freemasonry in Ireland is even scarcer than for England and Scotland. From a humorous speech given, in Latin, at Trinity College, Dublin, in 1688 it would seem that there was a lodge meeting within the university. In, or about, 1713 the Hon. Elizabeth St Leger is reported to have been made a Freemason upon overhearing the proceedings of a lodge being held in her father's, Viscount Doneraile's, house. Whether the story is true or not it seems to indicate that aristocrats were holding lodges in their houses. As all the early records of the Grand Lodge of Ireland have been lost it is not known when it was originally formed. The earliest record comes in *The Dublin Weekly Journal* for Saturday 26 June 1725. A lengthy article records that on 25 June the Grand Master, Grand Officers, and representatives of six Dublin lodges met, opened a Grand Lodge, and proceeded to elect *new* Grand Officers. This indicates that at least one previous Grand Lodge must have been held to elect the outgoing Grand Officers.

It would seem that initially the Grand Lodge of Ireland was a Dublin body; a Grand Lodge of Munster existed from at least December 1726. The two were merged in 1731 when James, 4th Lord Kingston became Grand Master of both. The merger appears to have been painless—efforts to hold meetings of the Grand Lodge of Munster in 1733 met with no

20 **Opposite**
Frederick Lewis, Prince of Wales 1707-51, son of George II.
Initiated 5 November 1737.

support. Like the English Grand Lodge, that of Ireland became a regulatory body superintending lodges throughout Ireland and, in 1730, published its own *Constitutions* based on the 1723 English *Constitutions*.

Despite the long existence of organized operative lodges and their admission of *accepted* members, the Scots did not form a Grand Lodge until 1736. The move was begun by four Edinburgh lodges and culminated in an assembly of the Masters and Wardens of thirty-two lodges at Mary's Chapel on 30 November 1736. A Grand Lodge was formed; William St Clair of Roslin was elected Grand Master; and various regulations were agreed for the conduct of the Grand Lodge. It is not known how many lodges existed in Scotland in 1736 but later events show that there were many more than the thirty-two attending the assembly. The Lodge Melrose St John maintained an independent existence until as late as 1891. Even within the founders of the Grand Lodge there was not total unity. The Lodge of Aitchisons Haven withdrew in 1737 and remained independent until 1814. The Lodge Mother Kilwinning, which had been constituting daughter lodges before the formation of the Grand Lodge, withdrew its support in 1744, and from that date until it rejoined the Grand Lodge in 1807 constituted at least thirty-seven daughter lodges.

The apparent unity of the Grand Lodge of England was shattered in 1751 when a rival, now known as the Antients Grand Lodge, sprang up in London. Formed initially by Irish Masons who had been unable to gain admission to London lodges it was joined by English Masons who believed that the original Grand Lodge had departed from the 'old institutions' by altering the rituals as a result of the appearance of printed exposures. The Antients Grand Lodge rapidly developed into a formidable rival, erecting lodges both at home and abroad and establishing 'fraternal correspondence' with the Grand Lodges in Ireland and Scotland. Whilst there was official hostility between the two English Grand Lodges, neither recognizing the existence of the other or each other's members as regularly-made Masons, in practice the further removed from London the closer the relations between individual lodges. Even at the centre, and despite official pronouncements, prominent members of both Grand Lodges enjoyed membership of their rival's lodges.

The situation in England was exacerbated by the revival in 1761 of the old lodge at York which claimed to be the Grand Lodge of All England and further complicated matters by constituting the dissident members of the Lodge of Antiquity, London (one of the founding lodges of the original Grand Lodge) as the Grand Lodge South of the River Trent in 1779. Clearly, a situation in which Freemasonry was divided and Grand Lodges could spring up at a whim was far from ideal. By the late 1790s, when the two junior rivals had dropped into oblivion, attempts were made to bring about a union of the original and Antients Grand Lodges. Initially, there

21 **Opposite**
The Scald Miserable Masons held mock processions to vie with the annual procession to the Grand Festival by Grand Lodge.

The Weſtminſter Journal; or, New Weekly Miſcellany.

By THOMAS TOUCHIT, of Spring-Gardens, Eſq;

SATURDAY, May 8, 1742.

From my own Apartment in Spring-Gardens.

THO' I belong to neither of the Fraternities mention'd in the following Pieces, and therefore am little concern'd in their annual Diſputes, I think it my Duty, as a Watchman of the City of *Weſtminſter*, to preſerve the Memory of the late extraordinary Cavalcade, the like to which hath never happen'd ſince I have been in Office. As more ſolemn Proceſſions have of late Years been very rare, it cannot ſurely be taken amiſs, either by the *Free-Maſons* or the *Scald-Miſerables*, that I give ſo much Diſtinction to this. T. T.

The FREE-MASONS Downfall; or, The Reſtoration of the SCALD-MISERABLES.

The Remonſtrance of the Right Worſhipful the Grand-Maſter, Deputy *Grand-Maſter*, Grand-Wardens, *and Brethren of the moſt Ancient and Honourable* SOCIETY *of* SCALD-MISERABLE-MASONS.

 WHEREAS by our Manifeſto of laſt Year, dated from our Lodge in *Brick-ſtreet*, We did, in the moſt explicite Manner, vindicate the ancient Rights and Privileges of this Society, and by inconteſtable Arguments evince our ſuperior Dignity and Seniority to all other Inſtitutions, whether *Grand-Volgi, Gregorians, Hurlothrumbians, Ubiquarians, Hiccubites, Lumber-Troopers,* or *Free-Maſons*; yet, nevertheleſs, a few Perſons under the laſt Denomination, ſtill arrogate to themſelves the uſurped Titles of *Moſt Ancient and Honourable*, in open Violation of Truth and Juſtice,—ſtill endeavour to impoſe their falſe Myſteries (for a Premium) on the Credulous and Unwary, under Pretence of being Part of our Brotherhood, and ſtill are determin'd with Drums, Trumpets, gilt Chariots, and other unconſtitutional Finery, to caſt a Reflection on the primitive Simplicity and decent Oeconomy of our Ancient and Annual Peregrination: We think therefore proper, in Juſtification of Ourſelves, publicly to Diſclaim all Relation or Alliance whatſoever, with the ſaid Society of Free-Ma-

ſons, as the ſame muſt manifeſtly tend to the Sacrifice of our Dignity, the Impeachment of our Underſtanding, and the Diſgrace of our ſolemn Myſteries: And further, to convince the Public of the Candour and Openneſs of our Proceedings, We here preſent them with a Key to our Proceſſion; and that the rather, as it conſiſts of many Things Emblematical, Myſtical, Hieroglyphical, Comical, Satirical, Political, &c.

And whereas many, perſuaded by the Purity of our Conſtitution, the nice Morality of our Brethren, and the peculiar Decency of our Rites and Ceremonies, have lately forſook the groſs Errors and Follies of *Free-Maſonry*, are now become true *Scald-Miſerables*: It cannot but afford a moſt pleaſing Satisfaction to all who have any Regard to Truth and Decency, to ſee our Proceſſion increaſed with ſuch a Number of Proſelytes; and behold thoſe whoſe Vanity, but the laſt Year, exalted them into a borrowed Equipage, now condeſcend to become the humble Cargo of a Sand-Cart: But——*Magna eſt Veritas, & prævalebit.*

A KEY; or, Explanation of the Solemn and Stately PROCESSION of the SCALD-MISERABLE-MASONS, as it was martiall'd on Tuesday the 27th paſt, by their Scald Purſuivant, Black Mantle.

Set forth by Order of the Grand-Maſter PONEY.

Two *Tylers*, or *Guarders*,
IN yellow Cockades, and Liveries, being the Colour ordained for the Sword-Bearer of State. They, as youngeſt enter'd 'Prentices, are to guard the Lodge with a drawn Sword from all Cowens and Eves-droppers, that is, Liſteners, leſt they ſhould diſcover the incomprehenſible Myſteries of Maſonry.

A Grand Chorus of Inſtruments,
To wit. Four Sackbutts, or Cow's Horns; ſix Hottentot Hautboys; four tinkling Cymbals, or Tea-Caniſters, with broken Glaſs in them; four Shovels and

Bruſhes; two Double Baſs Dripping-pans; a Tenor Frying-pan; a Salt-box in Delaſol; and a Pair of Gut-Tubs.

Two Pillars, Jachin and Boaz,
After the Proportion and Workmanſhip of the famous ones in the Porch of *Solomon's* Temple.

Their Height, their Thickneſs, and their Capitals
Adorned with Lilly-work, Net-work, and Pomegranate-work. That on the Right being call'd *Jachin*, is the Cant or Bye-Word for the enter'd 'Prentices; that on the Left *Boaz*, being the ſame to the Fellow-Craft.

Three Pair of Stewards,
With their Attendants, in Red Ribands, being their Colour, in three Gut-Carts drawn by three Aſſes each, their Aprons being lined with red Silk, their Jewels pendant to red Ribands, and their Heads properly adorned with emblematical Caps.

The true Original Maſon-Lodge,
Upon which poor old *Hyram* made all his enter'd 'Prentices. The Maſons, for want of this, are forced to make ſomething like it with Chalk on the Floor whenever they take the Culls in; that is, when they have a

William H. White

AHIMAN REZON:
OR,
A Help to a Brother;
Shewing the
EXCELLENCY of SECRECY,
And the first Cause, or Motive, of the Institution of
FREE-MASONRY;
THE
PRINCIPLES of the CRAFT,
And the
Benefits arising from a strict Observance thereof;
What Sort of MEN ought to be initiated into the MYSTERY,
And what Sort of MASONS are fit to govern LODGES,
With their Behaviour in and out of the Lodge.

Likewise the
Prayers used in the *Jewish* and *Christian* Lodges,
The Ancient Manner of
Constituting new Lodges, with all the Charges, &c.

Also the
OLD and NEW REGULATIONS,
The Manner of Chusing and Installing *Grand-Master* and *Officers*,
and other useful Particulars too numerous here to mention.

To which is added,
The greatest Collection of MASONS SONGS ever presented to
public View, with many entertaining PROLOGUES and EPILOGUES;

Together with
SOLOMON's TEMPLE an ORATORIO,
As it was performed for the Benefit of
FREE-MASONS.

By Brother LAURENCE DERMOTT, Sec.

LONDON:
Printed for the EDITOR, and sold by Brother *James Bedford*, at the
Crown in St. *Paul's Church-Yard.*

MDCCLVI.

22
*Ahiman Rezon. The
Constitutions of the Antients
Grand Lodge compiled by their
Grand Secretary, Laurence
Dermott.*

JACHIN *and* BOAZ;

OR, AN

AUTHENTIC KEY

To the DOOR of

FREE - MASONRY.

Calculated not only for the Inftruction of every New-
Made MASON, but alfo for the Information of all
who intend to become BRETHREN.

CONTAINING,

I. A circumftantial Account of all the Proceedings in making a Mafon, with the feveral Obligations of an ENTERED APPRENTICE, FELLOW-CRAFT, and MASTER; and alfo the Sign, Grip, and Pafs-Word of each Degree; with the Ceremony of the Mop and Pail.

II. The Manner of opening a Lodge, and fetting the Craft to Work.

III. The *Entered Apprentice, Fellow-Craft* and *Mafter's Lectures*, verbatim, as delivered in all Lodges; with the Songs at the Conclufion of each Part.

IV. The Origin of Mafonry; Defcription of *Solomon*'s Temple; Hiftory of the Murder of the Grand Mafter *Hiram* by the three Fellow-Crafts; the Manner of the Affaffins being difcovered, and their Punifhment; the Burial of *Hiram* by King *Solomon*'s Order; with the Five Points of Fellowfhip, &c.

V. The Ceremony of the Inftalment of the Mafters of different Lodges on St. *John*'s Day.

VI. A fafe and eafy Method propofed, by which a Man may obtain Admittance into any Lodge without paffing thro' the Form required, and thereby fave a Guinea or two in his Pocket.

ILLUSTRATED WITH

An accurate Plan of the DRAWING on the Floor of a Lodge.

And interfperfed with Variety of NOTES and REMARKS, neceffary to explain and render the Whole clear to the meaneft Capacity.

By a GENTLEMAN belonging to the Jerufalem Lodge; a frequent Vifitor at the Queen's Arms, St. Paul's Church Yard; the Horn, in Fleet-Street; Crown and Anchor, Strand; and the Salutation, Newgate-Street.

Try me; prove me.

LONDON: Printed for W. NICOLL. And,
DUBLIN: Re-printed, and fold by DILLON CHAMBERLAINE, in Smock-Alley; and the reft of the Bookfellers.

1760-61.

23 **Above**
Robert Sinclare, Grand Master of the York Grand Lodge, 1782.

24 **Left**
Printed exposures of Masonic ritual began to appear in the 1720s. This example first appeared in 1760 and is still reprinted.

25 **Far left**
*Royal Arch apron hand painted
with symbols and figures
representing the officers of a
chapter. c.1790.*

*26
Henry, Duke of Cumberland
1745-90. The first Royal Grand
Master, 1782-90, in his Royal
Arch robes.*

*27
Antony ten Broeke in his regalia
as Master of the Caledonian
Lodge, London, 1766.*

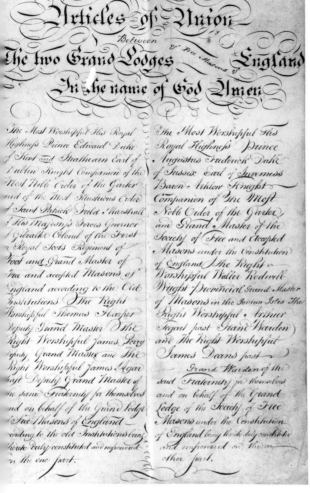

28
Articles of Union signed by the Dukes of Kent and Sussex and the negotiating teams of the premier and Antients Grand Lodge at Kensington Palace, 25 November 1813.

was little positive action and it was not until 1809 that negotiating committees were set up to bring about an equable union. Even then there appears to have been a reluctance on the part of an element within the Antients Grand Lodge and negotiations had reached a stalemate in 1813. Fate intervened with the resignation of the two Grand Masters. HRH George, Prince of Wales resigned as Grand Master of the original Grand Lodge on becoming Prince Regent and was succeeded by his younger brother HRH Augustus Frederick, Duke of Sussex. John, 4th Duke of Atholl, who had been Grand Master of the Antients Grand Lodge 1775-81 and again from 1791, resigned in November 1813 and was succeeded by HRH Edward, Duke of Kent. It says much for the authority of princes at that time that in a little over six weeks the two royal brothers had completed negotiations, formulated and received agreement to the

Articles of Union, and planned the great ceremonial which took place on 27 December 1813 by which the United Grand Lodge of England came into being with HRH the Duke of Sussex as Grand Master (Fig. 28).

By 1813 Freemasonry had become firmly established in the British Isles. The four Grand Lodges in England, Ireland, and Scotland, whilst following the same basic principles, had developed independently but harmoniously. Such was their early success that news of Freemasonry had spread abroad and between them the home Grand Lodges were to take Freemasonry around the world.

2
Freemasonry in Eighteenth-Century Europe

EUROPEAN Masonic scholars, like their English counterparts, spent much time attempting to link Freemasonry on the continent with operative stone masons and the gild system. The records of the German Steinmetzen and the French Compagnionage were avidly sought and searched for evidence of non-operatives having been admitted and having gradually taken over the trade organizations and converted them into Freemasonry. All to no avail. Many continental Masonic writers gave even freer rein to their imagination than did those of the English romantic school and gave birth to the ideas that Freemasonry had its origins in the Templars or Rosicrucians. Despite their writings there is no evidence that Freemasonry existed in continental Europe before the late 1720s.

In 1728 Philip, Duke of Wharton, who had been Grand Master of England 1722-3, set up a lodge in his apartment in Madrid. In April 1728 the lodge applied to the English Grand Lodge to be entered on the English register as a regular lodge. This application was followed by many others in the early 1730s setting up lodges in France, Germany and the Netherlands. Travellers and temporary residents took Freemasonry with them and established lodges without reference to any Grand Lodge. A good example is the English lodge in Florence (Fig. 30). Begun by expatriate English Masons about 1732 it attracted a number of foreign residents in the city and had begun to initiate Florentines when the first Papal Bull against Freemasonry was issued in 1738. The Italian members were questioned by the Inquisition and were forced to abjure their Freemasonry, but the foreign members continued to quietly hold their meetings.

Copy of the Deputation for Constituting a Lodge in Gibralter.

Kingston

Whereas application was lately made to our R^t Worship full Brother His Grace the most Noble Charles Lenox Duke of Richmond late Grand Master, by our Brother John Bailie Master, and Thomas Wilson and Benjamin Radenhurst Wardens of a Lodge of St Johns at Gibralter for and on the behalfe of several of our Brethren-Commission'd and non Commissioned Officers and others, representing That as they have nothing more at heart then their Duty to God, our King and Country, and to his Grace as Grand Master, They desire that they may be Constituted a regular Lodge in due fform. —————

These are therefore to Impower and authorize our welbeloved Brother John Bailie, Thomas Wilson, and Benjamin Radenhurst to convene our Brethren at Gibralter aforesaid and that they do in our place and Stead, Con: stitute a regular Lodge in due fform at Gibralter aforesaid (taking especial Care that they and every of them have been regularly made Masons) with like Priviledges as all other regular Lodges do enjoy, and that they be required to conform themselves to all and every the Regulations contained in the printed Constitutions and observe such other Rules and Instructions as shall from time to time be transmitted to them by us, or Nathaniel Blackerby Esqr our Deputy Grand Master, or the Grand Master, or his Deputy Grand Master for the time being, and that they do with the first Opportunity send to us, or our Deputy a List of the Members of their Lodge together with the Rules agreed on to be by them observed, to the end they may be entred in the Grand Lodge Book Given under our hand and Seal of Office at London this 9^h day of March 172⅞ and in the Year of Masonry 5728

By the Grand Master's Command

Nat: Blackerby Dep^y G. Master

J. Thornhill ⎫
M^r O'Connor ⎭ Grand Wardens

121

29
Deputation to constitute a lodge at Gibraltar, 9 March 1729, the first English lodge outside England.

30

*The Sackville Medal, 1733.
Charles Sackville visited
Florence in 1730 and appears to
have been a member of the
English Lodge there, who issued
this medal, the earliest known
Masonic medal.*

31
*The 'Jacobite' Lodge at Rome,
1735 was confined to expatriate
Scots. A page from the Minute
Book.*

A similar self-constituted lodge in Rome, organized by mainly Scottish Masons exiled for their part in the 1715 Jacobite rebellion, or their support of the Jacobite cause, gave rise to one of the enduring myths of Freemasonry—that much of early continental Freemasonry was Jacobite inspired and a means by which information was passed back to England to secret supporters of the Jacobite cause, ultimately leading to the 1745 rebellion led by Bonnie Prince Charlie. The myth reached the height of absurdity when it was claimed, four generations after the events, that not only was Charles Edward Stuart himself a Freemason but that in 1745 in Edinburgh he proclaimed himself Grand Master of the Masonic Knights Templar and issued a charter permitting the Order to meet in Scotland. The fact that the Masonic Knights Templar did not exist at that date and that the purported charter is an obvious forgery (amongst other things it refers to the Prince as Pretender to the throne of England and Scotland, a description he would never have put his signature to) are ignored by the conspiracy theorists. The lodge in Rome apart, there is no evidence for the fantasy that continental Freemasonry was a Jacobite organization.

The spread of Freemasonry in Europe was facilitated by three factors: the appointment of Provincial Grand Masters from England; lodges started from England becoming 'mother' lodges; and the issue of travelling warrants by the Grand Lodges of England, Ireland, and Scotland to lodges in regiments of the British Army.

The appointment of Provincial Grand Masters was personal to the Grand Master as the person appointed was to be his deputy and personal representative in the area defined by his patent of appointment. As the Grand Master's deputy the Provincial Grand Master was given authority to constitute new lodges. Constitutionally, these events were to be reported back to London so that the lodges could be entered on the register and official list of lodges, but in practice, with the problems of travel and communication, many of the European lodges went out of existence or worked for many years before Grand Lodge became aware of them. Although abiding by the *Constitutions* and obeying Grand Lodge, the European Provinces, to all intents and purposes, were working as independent Grand Lodges. The succession of English Provincial Grand Masters in Europe was as follows:

Hanover

1730	— Der Thom
1755	Jobst Anthony Hinuber
1786	Prince Charles of Macklenburgstrelitz

Russia

1731	Capt. John Phillips
1740	Gen. James Keith
1772	Ivan Perplench Elagin

Netherlands
1735   John Cornelius Rademacher
1756   Louis Dagran

Upper Saxony
1737   Henry William Marschall
1765   Count John G. H. de Wethern

Geneva
1737   George Hamilton

Hamburg and Lower Saxony
1740   Matthias Albert Luttman
1759   Gottfried Jacob Jaenisch
1786   John Gottfried von Exter
1799   John Philip Beckmann

Savoy and Piedmont
1740   Marquis des Marches
1773   Count de Bernez

Denmark and Norway
1749   Count Christian Conrad Danneskjold Laurvig
1765   Charles Fulman
1793   Charles, Landgrave of Hesse Cassel

Minorca
1749   Lt. Gen. Sir James Adolphus Oughton

Westphalia
1744   Baron George Augustus Hammerstein

Brunswick
1764   Ernest Sigmon de Leswitz
1770   Ferdinand, Duke of Brunswick

Italy
1766   Nicholas de Manuzzi

Rhineland and Franconia
1766   John Peter Gogel
1789   Johann Peter Leonhardi
1793   John Charles Bronner

Electorate of Saxony
1767   Aloys Peter d'Agdolo

Austrian Netherlands
1770   Francis, Marquis de Gages

Naples and Sicily
1770   Caesar Pignatelli, Duke of Rocca

Poland
1781   Count Halsen

Bavaria
1806   Prince Charles of Thurn and Taxis

The 'mother' lodge system was unconstitutional but, probably because of distance from London and difficulties of communication, was not interfered with. The authority given by the Grand Lodge of England to its lodges abroad was the same as to its home lodges: it was simply authority to meet as a lodge, make Freemasons, and elect successive officers of the lodge. The Masters of a number of English lodges, particularly in France and Prussia, began to act more like Provincial Grand Masters and issued dispensations to groups of Masons to meet as lodges. In due time these lodges became permanent lodges owing allegiance not to the Grand Lodge in London but to the local 'mother' lodge which had originally allowed them to meet. The English Lodge at Bordeaux is a typical example. Constituted on 17 April 1732, but not appearing on the register until 1766, as a lodge of mainly English merchants in Bordeaux, from 1740 it began to constitute other lodges in Bordeaux, Brest, Limoges, Paris, Cayenne, Cognac, Perigueux, and New Orleans. Although none of these actions was reported back to London, the English Lodge continued its link with the Grand Lodge in London and in all other

32
Plea for assistance by Michael Devon, Deputy Grand Secretary, 1769. An engraver of documents, Devon decorated patents, warrants and the Grand Lodge Minutes in the same style as his petition.

33
Francis, Duke of Lorraine, made a Freemason at The Hague, 1731, by a group of English Freemasons with authority from the Grand Lodge. He married Maria Theresa of Austria.

respects conducted itself as a typical English lodge until it became involved in the promotion of additional Masonic degrees, the development of which is described later in this chapter.

Military lodges with travelling warrants were, perhaps, to have more success in the colonies, but nevertheless they gave a certain impetus to the spread of Freemasonry in Europe, principally by the example being copied by the Grand Orient of France which warranted many lodges in the French army. The usual practice was, and is, for a lodge's warrant to specify where the lodge will hold its meetings. This obviously would not work with a military lodge as regiments were regularly on the move. The travelling warrant was devised to enable the lodge to meet wherever the lodge was stationed. Constitutionally, these lodges could only meet with the agreement of the colonel of the regiment and were permitted to draw

34
*French engraving c.1740
showing the reception of a
Fellowcraft.*

their members only from the regiment. Inevitably, this limited the number of members and military lodges began to admit civilians, initially from the people who serviced the regiment. When the regiment moved on, the civilians remaining would then apply to one of the British Grand Lodges for authority to meet, and so the number of lodges increased.

Being physically separated from England, and having a large degree of Masonic independence, it was not long before lodges in Europe began to seek total self-government. A Grand Lodge of France had appeared in the mid 1730s but as it was composed of self-constituted lodges and lodges which had evolved under the mother lodge system its appearance, like those of the Grand Lodges of Ireland and Scotland, appears to have been accepted without comment by the English Grand Lodge. Such was not the case in the Netherlands where an English Province had been established and was in a well-organized and flourishing state.

The Dutch, always fiercely independent, regarded their Province as allied to but independent of the English Grand Lodge and in 1756 declared themselves an independent Grand Lodge. The English Grand Lodge refused to acknowledge their independence and the argument rumbled on until 1770 when England recognized the independence of the Dutch Grand Lodge. The formal agreement between the two was to have an importance for future recognition of other Grand Lodges as it established the territorial sovereignty of the Dutch Grand Lodge within the acknowledged boundaries of the Netherlands, the English Grand Lodge regarding it as closed territory into which it could not introduce new lodges.

The situation in Germany was much more complicated as a result of Germany being not one nation but a collection of kingdoms, principalities, and electorates. As has been seen, English Provincial Grand Masters had been appointed for various parts of Germany throughout the eighteenth century. There were flourishing Provincial Grand Lodges in Hamburg (1740), Hanover (1755), and Frankfurt-am-Main (1766). In 1741 three English lodges in Saxony formed a Grand Lodge based in Dresden. In 1740 Frederick the Great (Figs. 38-9) formed a lodge in Berlin which assumed the status of a Grand Lodge in 1744 as the Grand National Mother Lodge of the Three Globes. It was followed by another Prussian Grand lodge in 1770, the Grand Land Lodge of Freemasons organized by Zinnendorf and using the Swedish Rite of Freemasonry. With the exception of Hamburg, Frankfurt-am-Main, and Hanover most of the Freemasonry in Germany had been imported from France through aristocratic circles. The various Grand and Provincial Grand Lodges had no regard for boundaries and set up new lodges all over the German states.

Masonic development in Scandinavia followed a completely different course to that in the rest of Europe. It had been introduced into Sweden,

35 Opposite
The Freemasons' Feast. French engraving c.1740. Conviviality and music making were very much a part of 18th-century Freemasonry.

Denmark, and Norway from England and Germany. Initially, after following the simple English Craft rituals the Swedish lodges gradually absorbed facets of the growing additional degrees developing in France and Germany, transforming them into a coherent rite of eleven degrees which, after the first three Craft degrees, is intensely Christian in content. In Sweden, Freemasonry has always enjoyed the patronage of the royal house, the king usually being Grand Master, and the 11th degree of the Swedish Rite, in addition to conferring the highest Masonic honour upon a recipient, is also a civil honour equivalent to English knighthoods.

The success of Freemasonry in Europe begs the question of why what was perceived to be a social and charitable society, reputedly a continuation of a medieval trade organization, should have appealed to a wide cross section of men in other countries? The answer, we believe, lies

36 **Left**
French engraving c.1740. The symbols would be drawn on the floor or painted onto a floor-cloth, then removed at the end of the ceremony.

37 **Above**
Treaty between the English and Dutch Grand Lodges, 1770, recognizing the independence and territorial sovereignty of the Dutch lodges.

in the basic principles of Freemasonry, Brotherly Love, Relief, and Truth, and the Masonic ideals of equality and freedom of thought. Society in much of eighteenth-century Europe was rigidly stratified, with little mobility between classes. Despite being the Age of Enlightenment it was also the era of the so-called benevolent despots. In many cases it would seem that Europeans wrongly equated Masonic ideals with political ideals of Liberty, Fraternity, and Equality and saw Freemasonry as a means of gaining an equality they could not achieve in their daily lives. This wrong equation and the unscrupulous misuse of Freemasonry by certain groups also led to the conspiracy theory linking Freemasonry with the French and other revolutionary movements. Whatever the original appeal of Freemasonry, the simple Craft ceremonies introduced from Britain did

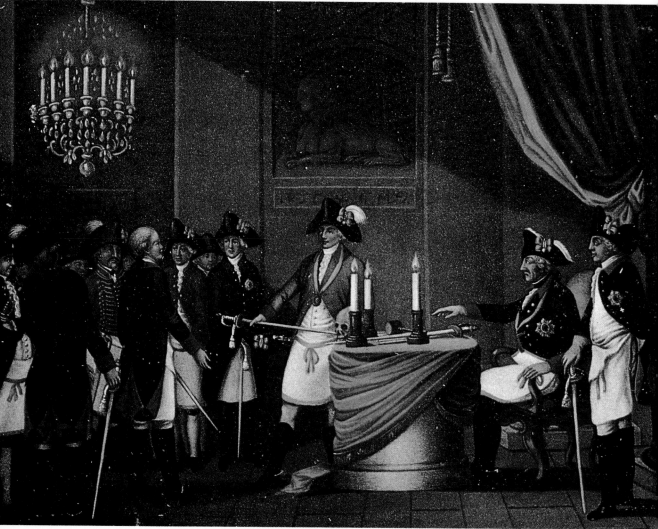

38 **Far left**
Frederick the Great. Initiated in 1739, he was later claimed as the authority for the Grand Constitutions of the Ancient and Accepted Rite.

39 **Far left**
Frederick the Great making the Margrave of Brandenburg a Mason, 1740.

40 **Left**
Meissen porcelain figure of a Freemason. By Kaendler, 1745.

not long hold an appeal for continental minds, which soon began to devise more and more complex rites, many of which bore no relation to or connection with the original simplicity of British Craft Freemasonry.

As Freemasonry spread throughout Europe, so its structure changed: the three Craft degrees remained, of course, essential and inviolate, but added to them was a profusion of additional degrees—innovations which began in France as the *Hauts Grades* but which spread rapidly into other countries, sometimes in unaltered form, sometimes dramatically changed. At first sight there seems to have been no end to the number and variety of these Rites and degrees; and when they are carefully recorded, as was done in 1861 by the French Masonic author, J. M. Ragon (Fig. 44), the figures are startling: '[Ragon] listed the names of more than 1400 "degrees" as well as a catalogue of seventy-five kinds of "Masonry", fifty-two Rites, thirty-four quasi-Masonic Orders, twenty-six androgynous Orders (i.e. admitting women) and six "Masonic Academies".'

On analysis, however, this seemingly bewildering variety reduces to two basic types of Rite: those made up of what are called *Ecossais* degrees, and those composed of Templar degrees (which are essentially a refinement of certain *Ecossais* grades). In addition to these two groups of chivalric degrees there were many idiosyncratic, esoteric offshoots stressing specific metaphysical doctrines such as alchemy or theurgy, and other quasi-Masonic rites and orders usually of an occult or overtly political nature.

But what were the impulses that lay behind this wholesale creation of degrees? Initially, there was the élitist attitude of the sophisticated aristocrats who comprised a significant part of French Masonry and acted as its driving force. For them the simplicity of the Craft degrees, whose legends are built around the symbolic activities of mere artisans, was inadequate; what they demanded—and created for themselves—were extravagant rituals with a more complex structure, more pomp, and a surfeit of high-sounding titles for those who participated in the ceremonies: High Priests, Knights, Princes, and Kings. Separate from this—and noticeable especially in Germany—was a reaction against the enlightenment and its rationalism; coupled with this was a burgeoning of hermetic and mystical groups who sought to give their ideas symbolic (and occasionally practical) expression within the framework of a Masonic Rite.

The *Ecossais* grades came into being through the élitism of French Masonry, but other factors, not always easily identifiable, played a significant role in their expansion and survival. It is impossible to analyse here all of these—social and political rivalries and the essential place of ritual in the human psyche among them—and we shall concentrate on their structure and historical development.

In common with those of all Masonic degrees at the time, the

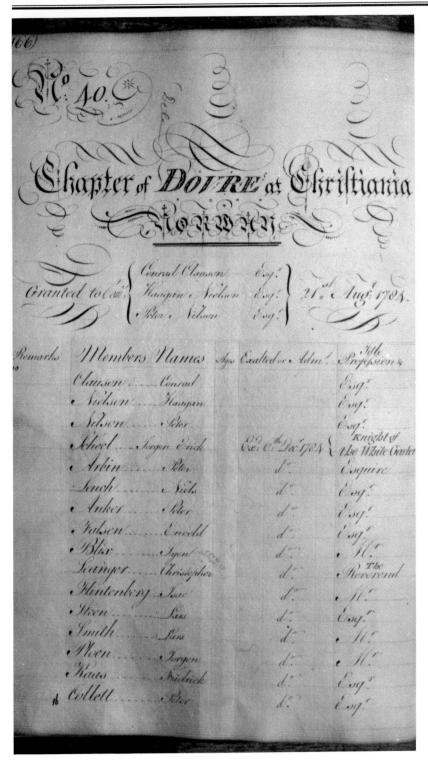

41
The Dovre Chapter at
Christiania was constituted in
London in 1784, then
immediately removed to
Norway.

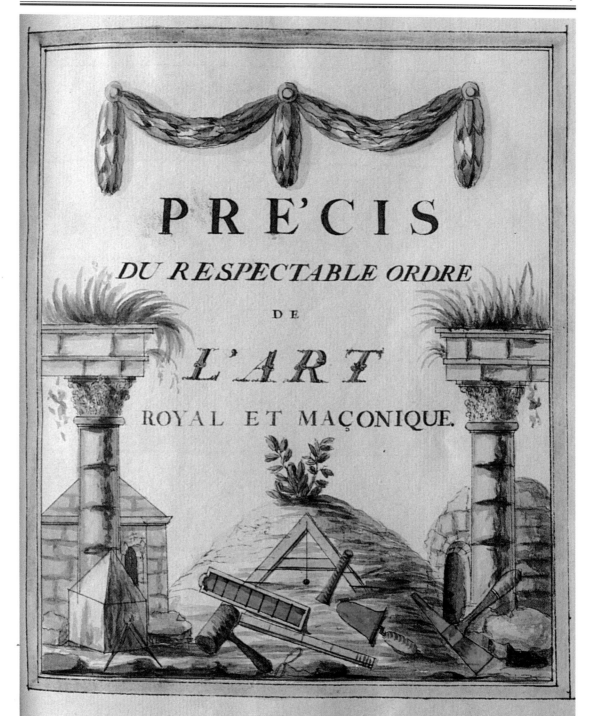

ceremonies of the *Ecossais* degrees were concerned with the symbolic building and rebuilding of the successive Temples at Jerusalem. That this was so is known from printed French 'exposures' of Masonry that first appeared in 1744. In one of them, *Le Parfait Maçon*, the author states that, 'Instead of weeping over the ruins of the Temple of Solomon, as their brethren do, the *Ecossais* are concerned with rebuilding it', and he goes on to give their 'historical' justification: 'It is from this great event that the *Ecossais* derive the epoch of their institution, and although they are later than the other Masons by several centuries, they consider themselves of a superior grade.' A catechism for the degree of *Ecossais* Master follows, together with a detailed description of the legend of the degree, showing marked similarities with later English Royal Arch rituals and supporting the idea of a common inspiration for all additional degrees.

But why were these degrees known as *Ecossais*? From where does the notion of a specific 'Scots Masonry' come? It can be traced to that fountainhead of all additional degrees, Ramsay's 'Oration', which if not the cause of the *Hauts Grades* certainly inspired their content. Ramsay claimed, as we have seen, that Freemasonry began as a chivalric order in the Holy Land, but he also argued for a strong Scottish connection:

At the time of the last Crusades many lodges were already erected in Germany, Italy, Spain, France and from thence, in Scotland because of the close alliance between the French and the Scots. James, Lord Steward of Scotland, was Grand Master of a Lodge established at Kilwinning in the west of Scotland 1286, shortly after the death of Alexander III, King of Scotland, and one year before John Baliol mounted the throne. This Lord received as Freemasons into his Lodge, the Earls of Gloucester and Ulster, the one English; the other Irish.

By degrees, our Lodges and Rites were neglected in most places. That is why, of so many historians, only those of Great Britain speak of our Order. Nevertheless, it preserved its splendour among those Scotsmen to whom the Kings of France confided during many centuries the safeguard of their royal person.

This association with Scotland—utterly spurious though it was—and the linking of Masonry with Christian chivalry appealed both to the French catholics (who did not approve of Deism) and to the Jacobite exiles in France whose cause it helped to glamorize. Indeed, the Masonic historian Paul Naudon argued that:

Nothing is more certain than that the Stuarts and the Jesuits, who were their best supporters, used the *Ecossais* Masonic lodges whose respect for tradition and for Catholicism served their cause: and that the high degrees favoured this action.

Perhaps because of the Jacobite connections—and certainly after the failure of the 1745 Rebellion—the *Ecossais* degrees made little, if any, headway in England and were confined to continental Europe.

42 **Opposite**
Title page of an important French MS. c.1760, giving details of many Masonic degrees then practised.

43 Far left
One of the many watercolour
plates illustrating the 'Précis'
MS. This is for the Craft
degrees.

44
J.M. Ragon in his regalia as a
member of the Royal Order of
Scotland. Watercolour portrait
by his son.

45
The Lodge Room at Rouen of
the Perfect Union Lodge.
Engraved by M. Desmaisons.

As new degrees proliferated, the *Ecossais* degrees were absorbed into Rites and systems of degrees of which they formed an important part but not the whole. From manuscript and printed rituals of the 1750s and 1760s it is possible to analyse the structure of such Rites and to arrive at a division of early high degrees according to their symbolism and moral purpose. A. L. F. Jackson, in his book *Rose Croix* (1987, 2nd edition) has tabulated them as follows:

(a) Those dealing with the replacement of Hiram and the completion of King Solomon's Temple. They seem designed to teach the symbolical lesson that every man must make his own spiritual temple.

(b) The 'vengeance' group concerned with elaborating that part of the story in the Traditional History of the Third Degree which deals with the finding and punishment of the assassins, and the rewarding of their captors. The titles of this group often include the word *Elu* (Elect) [As Brigadier Jackson goes on to point out, it is difficult to draw *any* high moral purpose from such degrees.]

(c) The rebuilding of the Temple by Zerubbabel and the search for lost secrets in the foundations of the old building. They seem to symbolize man's search for his personal divinity.

(d) Degrees conferring powers of inspection and discipline. [Within the Rite, that is.]

(e) The Philosophical, Templar and Christian degrees.

A detailed list comparing the degrees of merely the more important Rites is beyond the scope of the present work, and it would serve little purpose save to confuse the reader; but for those who desire it, an attempted classification is given as an Appendix in A. E. Waite's *The Secret Tradition in Freemasonry* (1937).

Containing as it did the more worthwhile elements of the *Hauts Grades* and displaying, perhaps as a consequence, a surprising resilience, *Ecossais* Masonry flourished while other additional degrees languished. Throughout the eighteenth century it grew in both stature and membership (although its fortunes in France were chequered) and eventually developed, after passing through a succession of more or less radical reconstructions, into the present-day Ancient and Accepted Scottish Rite.

The first attempt at organizing and controlling the *Ecossais* degrees seems to have been made at Bordeaux in the 1740s, but the Rite ostensibly controlled by the Mother Lodge there was by no means the only one active in France, and the first clear indication of an organized rite with any real degree of central control comes in a document of 1761. In that year Stephen Morin, a French merchant born in the West Indies (or in New York according to other authorities), received a patent from the council of the 'Grand and Sovereign Lodge of St Jean de Jerusalem' (and

46
*French Rose Croix apron
c.1830. Ink and watercolour
design from a regalia maker's
pattern book.*

47
A collection of French 19th century Rose Croix jewels in paste and brilliants. The central emblems of the degree are the rose, Calvary Cross and Pelican.

by inference from the Grand Lodge of France) appointing him 'Grand Inspector in all parts of the New World' and granting him power to found a personal lodge wherever he happened to be—this in order to 'Multiply the Royal Order of Masonry in all the Perfect and Sublime Degrees'.

Morin did not reach the West Indies until 1763 as he was captured at sea by the British during his voyage in 1761, but when he arrived he set about taking control (or attempting so to do) of the Higher Degrees although the patent did not specifically give him such powers and in 1766 the Grand Lodge of France revoked his authority as Grand Inspector. Nothing daunted, Morin created his own 'Rite of Perfection' of 25 degrees (more properly the 'Rite of Sublime Princes of the Royal Secret'), organizing it on the basis of Constitutions of 1762 that he seems to have compiled himself while drawing heavily on those of the Grand Lodge of France. In 1771 Morin died and his work was carried on first by Henry Francken—who brought the Rite to North America—and later by the Comte de Grasse-Tilly who was ultimately responsible for adding eight

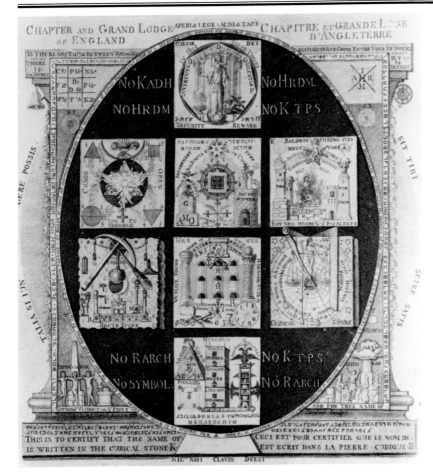

48
Engraved chart by Peter Lambert de Lintot for the Rite of Seven Degrees, which he introduced into England in the 1770s.

degrees to the Rite and setting up the Supreme Council at Charleston in 1800, from which the present 33-degree Scottish Rite derives. But here we must leave the story of the Scottish Rite until a later chapter and consider the fortunes of the other High Degrees in Europe.

The central feature of the Scottish Rite is the essentially Christian Eighteenth Degree of Rose-Croix, but its origins lie in German rather than French traditions. The first fully-fledged Rose-Croix ritual was developed in 1765 by J. B. Willermoz, a prominent Mason and occult enthusiast of Lyons, who drew upon the alchemical ideas of self-styled German Rosicrucians associated with the Rite of Strict Observance. This Rite, called originally 'Rectified Masonry', had been founded in 1755 by Karl Gotthelf Von Hund, a Saxon nobleman who was the foremost early propagator of the Templar myth in Freemasonry and an enthusiastic creator of Templar Rites.

Von Hund had an undoubted flair for organization and his Rite, which took the name 'Strict Observance' (to distinguish it from the 'lax

49 Far left
Symbolic chart for the Lodge of Perfect Observance No. 1 under the breakaway Grand Lodge South of the River Trent, which worked De Lintot's Rite of Seven Degrees.

50 Above
Emanuel Swedenborg 1688-1772. His membership of Freemasonry has never been proved, but his ideas were adopted by some Masonic systems and led to the developments of the short-lived Swedenborgian Rite of Freemasonry in the 19th century.

51 Left
Wolfgang Amadeus Mozart 1756-91. Initiated in Vienna, he was to compose music for the Viennese Lodges. Vienna porcelain statuette.

observance' of the three-degree system of English Craft Masonry) in 1764, rapidly expanded throughout Germany. The Rite was tightly structured and well disciplined: 'brethren were dubbed Knights, received Latin-names and pledged themselves to unquestioning obedience to the commands of Hund'. It also appealed to the vanity of its members with its sumptuous ceremonies and gorgeous regalia (Figs. 46-7):

The Strict Observance proved very attractive. When the candidate had passed through the three degrees and that of the 'Scottish Master', and had particularly distinguished himself, he was elevated to the 'Inner Order' in which he first became a novice or 'Chevalier de l'aigle', then Knight Templar, and finally *eques professus*. The Knights of the 'Inner Order' no longer met in Lodges but in Chapters. Over their purple-coloured knightly garb and the gold-embroidered rosettes was thrown the white cloak bearing the red cross of the Knights Templars. The Order aroused their deep enthusiasm, and they threw themselves heart and soul into their work.

In its essence the Strict Observance was an epitome of the 'hermetic' reaction of many Freemasons to the materialism of the Enlightenment: an attempted revival of the Knights Templars who were perceived as custodians of secret doctrines and as the true source of both Masonic ritual and Masonic symbolism. Nor was this all; behind Von Hund lay, or so he claimed, the 'Unknown Superiors', chief of whom was Prince Charles Edward Stuart, the Young Pretender. (He, of course, knew nothing of this and when taxed with the matter in 1777 denied any involvement with any form of Freemasonry: the Unknown Superiors were a figment of Von Hund's imagination.) None the less, from the august body, filtered through that same fertile imagination, the members of the Rite received the secrets of alchemy.

The Rite was further enriched in 1767 by another stream from the Templar fountain: the Order of Clerks Templar that had descended—or so its creator, the Protestant pastor J. A. Starck, claimed—from the Templar Priests, the clergy of the Order who alone had known its true esoteric secrets. But after an uneasy association for some years the Clerical Templars broke away from the Strict Observance, although the loss of Starck and his followers was more than offset by the arrival of Willermoz who, having joined the Rite in 1774, took it up and, as far as that part of it he effectively controlled from Lyons was concerned, transformed it by the introduction of the doctrines of Martines de Pasqually and Louis Claude de Saint-Martin (which are given in outline below).

Von Hund had ceased to be the Superior of the Strict Observance in 1772 when control passed to the Duke of Brunswick, but the Rite continued to expand until Von Hund's death in 1776 and the final breach with Starck in the following year. From then on the increasingly complex history of the Rite is one of gradual disintegration (a state of affairs not

52
The Chevalier d'Eon. A French spy condemned to dress as a woman for much of his life, d'Eon was made a Mason in London in 1768.

untypical of the *Hauts Grades*) until the official Congress (or Convent, as it was called) at Wilhelmsbad in 1782. Here the Rite was completely reorganized and effectively transformed into Willermoz's creation, the *Rite Ecossais Rectifié* and the *Chevaliers Bienfaisant de la Cité Saint*, which both preserved the tradition of chivalry but cast off Templarism. The centre of Masonic chivalry thus returned to France, but it was to be overwhelmed by the Revolution and Willermoz's Rite was destined to survive, more or less intact, only in Switzerland.

It must here be stressed that this is very much a simplified account of the extremely convoluted history of the Strict Observance, and it should also be borne in mind that none of these 'higher' Rites and Orders acted in isolation: theirs was a continuing story of unions, schisms, dissolutions, and rebirths, and of a regular shifting of allegiances by members as each new Rite arose and presented its own 'true' interpretation of Masonry. Fascinating though all of them are, it will suffice to describe only a few of the more interesting: Pasqually's 'Elect Cohens', Cagliostro's Egyptian Rite of Masonry, and the quasi-Masonic Order of the Illuminati—a body that was destined to excite the fears, and what passes for the intellect, of every hysterical anti-Mason both then and at every period since.

53
Joseph Balsamo, self-styled Count Cagliostro and inventor of the Egyptian Rite of Freemasonry, which he demonstrated all over Europe.

Martines de Pasqually, born at Grenoble in 1710, seems to have begun his Masonic activities in the 1750s and to have established his *Rite des Elus Coens* (or Elect Priests) at Toulouse in 1760. The Rite soon spread to other French cities—notably Bordeaux, Lyons, and Paris, where its governing body, or Sovereign Tribunal, resided—and rapidly gained converts to its curious doctrines. There were nine degrees within the Rite, three for each of its divisions: the Porch contained three degrees that corresponded to those of Craft Masonry, and these were followed by three other symbolic degrees of the Temple; above and beyond were those of the Shrine—the degree of the *Réaux-Croix* (a baffling name supposedly derived from Hebrew: it did *not* mean 'True Cross'). Although Pasqually's esoteric doctrines, which were based on gnosticism and on the Cabbala, were made plain from the outset their practical application was reserved for the Shrine.

Man, argued Pasqually, must understand the manner of the soul's descent into matter (and thus captivity) before he can learn how to liberate it and thus to unite himself with the Divine. This complex process was known as 'Reintegration' and its final stages, as far as the individual was concerned, took place in the ceremonies of the highest degree in which, by means of magical evocation, not only was the initiate enabled to see and to unite himself with this 'guardian angel' but was also permitted to see the 'Repairer' (Jehoshua, or Jesus) who appeared in person. But this was not the final goal of 'Reintegration', which looked beyond the individual to the salvation of *all* intelligent beings, both on Earth and throughout the universe.

This curious fusion of Freemasonry, magic, and gnostic doctrine carried on its work until 1774 when Pasqually died at Port-au-Prince in what is now Haiti. The Rite was then taken over by Willermoz who, as Provincial Chancellor of the *Directoire d'Auvergne*, absorbed it into the Strict Observance, adding to it the theological doctrines of Saint-Martin, who had brought order and orthodoxy (of a kind) to the ideas of Pasqually. Ultimately, Martinist ideas—filtered through Willermoz—passed into the Rite of the *Chevaliers Bienfaisant de la Cité Saint* while the *Elus Coens* vanished utterly.

Saint-Martin was unusual among esoteric Masons of his day in that he neither wished for nor established any form of Rite or Order to propagate his doctrines. His attitude was in marked contrast to that of Giuseppe Balsamo who, as Count Alessandro Cagliostro, gloried in elaborate rituals and desired nothing more than to found a Rite of his own.

Cagliostro (Fig. 53) is perceived almost universally as a charlatan, but it should be noted that he genuinely believed in the alchemy, mediumship, and other esoteric doctrines that he espoused and taught. He was born at Palermo, Sicily, in 1743 and while still a young man took up his occult pursuits during the course of a visit to Malta. In 1776 Cagliostro, now married, came to London where, according to his own account, he was initiated into Freemasonry in the Esperance Lodge. He then travelled about Europe visiting Masonic lodges and perfecting his magical practices, eventually arriving in 1779 in Courland (now Latvia) where he introduced his 'Egyptian Rite' of Masonry, with himself as the Grand Cophta. This was, so he claimed, the only true Masonry, Craft Masonry having degenerated and become incomplete through its exclusion of women; the Egyptian Rite, however, admitted women—albeit in separate 'Lodges of Adoption' and using different rituals from those reserved for men. For both men and women there were three grades (of Apprentice, Companion, and Master) corresponding to the three Craft degrees, and much of the symbolism of the Egyptian Rite was derived from Craft Masonry—with the addition of alchemical, astrological, cabbalistic, and magical elements and a profusion of stylized Egyptian symbols.

The third grade ceremony was little more than a magical ritual. After an elaborate preamble, which included invocations of the planetary spirits, the 'Dove of the Rite'—a young boy or girl—was hypnotized and put into a state of alleged clairvoyance in which he or she would prophesy, see visions, and pronounce upon the candidate's fitness. All this while Cagliostro carried out the procedures of a ceremony of ritual magic.

Such an extravaganza (every ceremony involved the most elaborate furnishings and regalia) was assured of success and for some years lodges of the Egyptian Rite flourished throughout Europe, especially in France, until 1785 and the scandal of Marie Antoinette's stolen necklace. Cagliostro was unjustly implicated, imprisoned, and when finally released, banished from France. He went first to England (Fig. 54) but gained little support, and then wandered about Europe until 1789 when he visited Rome—only to be arrested by the Inquisition and tried for heresy, sorcery, sacrilege, and other offences. Being found guilty he was sentenced to death, but this was commuted to life imprisonment in the fortress of San Leo at Urbino where he died in 1795. Without its Grand Cophta, for whose benefit it existed, the Egyptian Rite could not survive and when Cagliostro died his Rite died with him.

Among Cagliostro's most heinous crimes, at least in the eyes of the papacy, was that of Freemasonry, an institution that it both hated and feared. To make matters worse, he was also accused of being a member of another order that was viewed by Rome with even greater alarm: the Order of the Illuminati.

Created in 1776 by Adam Weishaupt, a Professor of Law at the University of Ingoldstadt in Bavaria, the Order of the Illuminati (or Enlightened Ones) was an avowed secret society dedicated to fighting against religious and secular tyranny and for the reformation of society on

wholly democratic lines. Weishaupt recognized the difficulty of rapidly implanting the decidedly unfashionable aims of egalitarianism and rationalism in his followers and designed the structure of the order so that these ends only gradually became apparent. The initiate, who was required to take an oath of strict secrecy and unquestioning obedience as well as a pledge renouncing all ties to family and friends, was led by stages towards the secret doctrines of the Order by way of a careful programme of instruction in the works of classical moralists and of the contemporary 'Philosophes' and materialists.

Having entered the first grade of Novice, the initiate was further

54
Cagliostro demonstrated his Rite to the Lodge of Antiquity No. 1 in London in 1786 and was lampooned by 'a brother Mason, witness of the scene'.

required to undertake regular self-examination and to report on the doings of his mentor in the order (thus enabling Weishaupt to nip rebellion in the bud). Once he had given satisfaction of his work the initiate could proceed through the higher grades of Minervale and Minervale Illuminatio, all the while advancing in knowledge but remaining ignorant of the identity of the order's founder, its membership, and its true aims. Beyond these grades lay the Areopagus, a secret inner circle of the rulers of the Order who were aware of the ultimate goal of the revolutionary transformation of society, which goal was principally to be sought by infiltrating the upper echelons of society and gaining positions of power and influence. This theory was by practice.

The Order had begun, with five members, but after three years of intensive effort they had grown to only 54, scattered throughout five centres, or 'colonies', in Bavarian cities. Many of the members, originally attracted to a quasi-religious society that would satisfy their yearnings for

55
Music was an important part of a lodge meeting, and many German and French Masonic song books were published.

AUSWAHL von Maurer Gesängen

mit Melodien der vorzüglichsten Componisten in zwey Abtheilungen getheilt;

gesammlet und herausgegeben, von F. W. Böheim.

Berlin, 1798.

changing the world, had relished the secrecy and the use of 'democratic' pseudonyms (Weishaupt, for example, was known as Spartacus). There was also an undoubted demand among 'advanced' circles in Bavaria for literature that was, in one way or another, subversive of the religious and political establishment—literature that was freely available elsewhere in Germany where freedom of thought was not stifled. But they demanded more enlightenment than Weishaupt gave them and fretted increasingly under his dictatorial control.

To resolve this crisis of confidence Weishaupt decided on action: the Order would infiltrate Freemasonry and draw recruits from Masonic lodges. Thus the Order of the Illuminati became the first society dedicated to political revolution that attempted, cynically in this case, to use Masonic secrecy as a means to its own ends—and its attempt was successful. Or so it seemed.

After taking control of a Lodge at Munich in 1779, the Order sought and obtained—from the Grand Lodge Royal York at Berlin—authority to found daughter lodges. These were soon spread across southern Germany and Austria and by 1782 membership had risen to 300. This success in Masonic circles was largely due to the efforts of Adolf Francis, Baron Knigge, who had joined Weishaupt in 1779 and was soon taken into his confidence. But Knigge's approach to promoting the Order was to be very different: he rejected Weishaupt's obsessive anti-clerical attitudes as inappropriate to the world outside Bavaria, and demanded structural reforms which were implemented in 1781. Weishaupt's autocratic rule was replaced by an oligarchy and the system of grades was dramatically expanded, attaining its final form in the following year. The existing grades, with one addition, became those of a new preparatory Class of Initiates, followed by three degrees of symbolic Masonry and two of *Ecossais* Masonry in the Masonic Class; at the apex of the system was the Class of the Mysteries, consisting of the grades of Priest and Prince in the Lesser Mysteries, and of Magus and King in the Greater.

This reconstruction led to an even greater expansion of the Order, rising to a peak in 1784 when there were some 2,500 members. But its end was now in sight. Weishaupt had quarrelled with Knigge over the nature of the higher grades and accused him of distorting the aims of the Order by turning it to purely mystical ends. The quarrel could not be settled and in July 1784 Knigge left the Order. By this time, too, rumours were circulating publicly about the anti-social nature of the Order; Willermoz attacked in print attempts by the Illuminati to subvert the Strict Observance at the Convent of Wilhelmsbad (although he did not mention its name); and an ex-member had revealed its secrets—much embellished—to the Bavarian authorities, who promptly issued a decree in June 1784 forbidding membership of secret societies. This was followed by a further decree in March 1785 that specifically banned both the Illuminati and the Freemasons. A war of words immediately broke out and a flood of pamphlets appeared either attacking or defending the Order, to be followed by a detailed exposé of the wickedness of the Illuminati based upon Weishaupt's papers, which had been seized after he fled from Bavaria immediately before the edict banning his Order was issued.

The Order itself faded away, but its influence lived on, perpetuated by hysterical claims that it had been responsible for the excesses of the French Revolution. Even today professional anti-Masons draw upon this house of straw for evidence of the inherent wickedness of Freemasonry—conveniently forgetting that the Order of the Illuminati had imposed on and manipulated Freemasonry just as cynically as it used everything else that came within its orbit. Its greatest influence, however, has been on papal perceptions of the Craft, feeding the hostility which has led the Church of Rome to be ever the most implacable opponent of Freemasonry and the most assiduous in her attempts to crush it.

The first papal condemnation of Freemasonry came in 1738 (Fig. 56), but it was not the first official attack to be made upon the Craft. *That* had taken place in 1735 in Holland where Masons at Amsterdam had been assaulted by a mob. This led to the setting-up of a Commission of Inquiry, which reported unfavourably on the Craft so that an edict was issued forbidding Masonic assemblies. It soon, however, fell into disuse. Similar proscriptions of Freemasonry occurred in France (confined effectively to Paris) in 1737 and 1744, and in Geneva (1744) and Berne (1745), although none were of long duration. In each case the authorities were concerned at possible public disturbances and official jockeying for position also played its part—there is no hint at all of fears of political or religious subversion; nor were any of these actions in response to papal condemnations.

Much is made in anti-Masonic circles of the first formal condemnation of Freemasonry by Pope Clement XII in his Bull *In eminenti*, and it is as well to examine it carefully. The Bull excommunicated all members of the Craft and reserved powers of absolution to the Pope alone. Much of the text concerns the supposed moral justification of the prohibition and outlines its specific parameters. The essential part is the first section:

It has come to our knowledge and indeed it is a matter of public notoriety, that there has been a great development, spreading far and wide and growing in strength from day to day, of certain Societies, Meetings, Clubs, Reunions, Conventicles or Lodges, commonly known by the name of 'Liberi Muratori', 'Francs Maçons', or otherwise variously designated according to the local idiom, in which men of no matter what religion and sect, content with a certain affectation of natural virtue, are mutually banded together in a close and exclusive league, in accordance with laws and statutes which they have framed for themselves. Further they concert measures in secrecy and are bound under extravagant penalties by an oath taken on the Bible to shroud their activities in

Condemnatio Societatis, feù Conventicularum -- *de Liberi Muratori* -- aùt -- *de Francs Maſſons* -- ſub pœna Excommunicationis ipſo facto incurrendæ, ejus abſolutione excepto Mortis Articulo Summi Pontifici reſervata.

CLEMENS EPISCOPUS
SERVUS SERVORUM DEI.

Univerſis Chriſtifidelibus ſalutem, & Apoſtolicam Benedictionem

IN eminenti Apoſtolatus Specula, meritis licèt imparibus, Divina diſponente Clementia conſtituti iuxtà creditum NobisPaſtoralis providentiæ debitum jugi (quantum ex alto conceditur) ſolicitudinis ſtudio iis intendimus, per quæ erroribus, vitiiſque aditu intercluſo, Orthodoxæ Religionis potiſſimùm ſervetur integritas, atque ab univerſo Catholico Orbe difficillimis hiſce temporibus perturbationum pericula propellantur.

Sanè

56
Pope Clement XII's Bull against Freemasonry — In Eminanti — promulgated in 1738.

impenetrable silence. Since, however, it is of the very nature of wrong-doing to betray itself and to give itself away by the outcry which it raises, hence the aforesaid associations or assemblies have excited such vehement suspicion in the minds of the Faithful that to enrol oneself in these Lodges is in the judgement of men of sense and high principle tantamount to incurring the stigma of a libertine and miscreant; for assuredly if such people were not doing evil they would never have so much hatred of the light. Moreover their ill-repute had spread to such a degree that in very many countries the associations aforesaid have some time ago been proscribed by secular rulers and have been wisely suppressed as dangerous to the safety of the realm.

In brief, the Pope was condemning Freemasonry because it was a rapidly-growing, apparently clandestine society whose members were bound by an oath of secrecy; it had deistic tendencies, and it was viewed with suspicion by civil authorities who looked upon the members as being of evil repute. The papal motives for condemning the Craft can thus be seen as partly disciplinary but largely political, centring on fears of conspiracy that may well have been fuelled by Jacobite suggestions of Hanoverian (and thus by implication, anti-Catholic) influence in English Lodges at Rome and elsewhere in Italy. Some of Clement's reasons for this condemnation were kept back: in the second section of the Bull he refers to 'other just and reasonable motives known to us', but he does not elaborate on them.

Religious considerations were clearly secondary, although overt indifference to religion was anathema to the Church and the oath of secrecy was a clear threat to the Confessional. The greatest indifference, however, was shown by the secular authorities who did little to promulgate the Bull. Individual Masons *were* persecuted in places where the Bull was acted upon, such enforcement being carried out by the Inquisition (more properly, the Holy Office); but only a few individuals were concerned. In addition, the English Lodge at Florence was suppressed, but no further papal action was forthcoming until 1751, when Pope Benedict XIV confirmed *In eminenti* in the Bull *Providas*. This was itself probably stimulated by the activities of a Jesuit, Fr. Pepe, who had tried to stir up anti-Masonic feeling in Naples, leading to a hostile edict banning Masonic meetings in the city; but the edict seems to have been a sop to papal susceptibilities and no action was taken against Neapolitan Freemasons, who saw the Craft flourish in their city.

Real hostility was found only where promulgation of the Bull was accompanied by repressive action on the part of the civil authorities. Thus at Florence the English Lodge was disbanded immediately upon the Bull's promulgation, and the Lodge's secretary, Tommasso Crudeli, was subsequently arrested and imprisoned by the Inquisition. For two years Crudeli remained in wretched conditions but although he was interrogated at length he was not, contrary to popular opinion, tortured. Nor did he

57/58 **Opposite**
Two scenes of the Portuguese Inquisition at work, used by John Coustos to illustrate his account of his persecution.

disclose to the Inquisition anything about Masonry that it did not already know. Eventually, in 1741, he was released.

Matters were worse in Spain where Freemasonry was outlawed in 1740 and a number of Masons sent to the galleys. A further edict against the Craft was issued in 1751, and to further its success a Franciscan friar, José Torrubia, obtained initiation under false pretences into a lodge at Madrid (after first receiving a papal dispensation in respect of the oath he would be obliged to take). Having thus perjured himself, Torrubia proceeded to deliver to the authorities a list of Masons whom he accused of being 'sodomites and magicians, heretics and atheists', adding for good measure that they 'should be burned at a devotional *auto-da-fé* for the glorification of the faith and the fortification of the faithful'. Happily his advice was not taken.

The most famous, or infamous, case of Masonic persecution by the Holy Office had, however, taken place some years before this in Portugal. The Bull had been issued at Rome on 28 April 1738 and was promulgated in Portugal within a matter of weeks, whereupon an Irish lodge at Lisbon decided to suspend its meetings and inform the Inquisition. An enquiry

59
John Coustos. Engraved
frontispiece to his book.

THE
SUFFERINGS
OF
JOHN COUSTOS,
FOR
FREE-MASONRY,

AND FOR

His refusing to turn ROMAN CATHOLIC,

IN THE

INQUISITION at *Lisbon*;

Where he was fentenc'd, during Four Years, to
the GALLEY; and afterwards releas'd from
thence by the gracious Interpofition of his
prefent Majefty King GEORGE II.

To which is annex'd,
The ORIGIN of the INQUISITION, with
its Eftablifhment in various Countries. A diftinct Account of that Tribunal, with many Examples of its In-
juftice and Cruelty; and the Practice of the PRIMITIVE
CHURCH, in bringing over Hereticks, compared with
that of the INQUISITION.

Extracted from a great Variety of the moft approved AUTHORS.

Enrich'd with SCULPTURES, defign'd by Mr. BOITARD.

Quid hoc majus poterat intendere accufator facerdos? fuit enim, fuit & hoc delato-
rum genus, qui nominibus antiftites, revera autem fatellites, atque adeo carnifices,
non contenti miferos evolviffe patrimoniis, calumniabantur in fanguinem, & vitas
premebant reorum jam pauperum.
Latinus Pacatus, in Panegyrico Theodofio dicto, Cap. xxix. p. m. 509.

LONDON:
Printed by W. STRAHAN, for the AUTHOR, 1746.

60
Title page of Coustos's book. The
book is now a valuable source
for information on Freemasonry
in the 1730s and 1740s.

took place in July 1738 at which the Inquisitors concluded that most of the members were good Catholics, that nothing contrary to faith or morals had taken place, and that the Masonic oath did not apply to matters of religion or the state. As the lodge had been disbanded, no further action was taken against the members—a course of action in marked contrast to what was to happen three years later.

In 1738 there were three lodges at Lisbon: the Irish Lodge, which disbanded itself; an English Lodge with a largely Protestant membership; and a Lodge of French Catholics whose Master was a diamond cutter, one John Coustos, a Swiss Protestant who had been brought to England as a boy and who was thus a British subject. A decree condemning Freemasons to death was issued in Portugal in 1743 and on 5 March of that year Coustos was arrested, having been denounced by a neighbour. He was brought before the Inquisition and when interrogated made a full confession of his Masonic activities, including a detailed account of the ritual (despite his protestations to the contrary in his published account, the Inquisition records show that Coustos *did* reveal the Masonic secrets). His confession notwithstanding, Coustos was later tortured on the rack, seemingly as a punishment for his crimes, and then sentenced to six years in the galleys. However, through the intervention of the British authorities he was released and in 1746 published *The Sufferings of John Coustos*, which led to an upsurge of public support for Freemasonry in England (Figs. 57-8).

It did not, however, put an end to anti-Masonry. The Jesuits in particular attacked the Craft, blaming it for their woes in Portugal, France, and Spain from 1759 onwards, and for their suppression in 1773. When their society was restored in 1814 their hostility continued. Other Roman Catholic orders also assailed Freemasonry, and in a sermon preached at Aix-la-Chapelle in 1778 a Capuchin, Fr. Schuff, introduced a new and hateful element into anti-Masonry—that of anti-semitism:

The Jews who crucified the Saviour were Freemasons, and Pilate and Herod were the wardens of a Lodge. Judas had been admitted a Mason in a Synagogue before he betrayed Christ, and when he gave back the thirty pieces of silver before setting out to hang himself, he did nothing more than pay the fee for initiation into the Order.

The upheavals of the French Revolution led to a disruption of Masonic activity in France but served only to encourage anti-Masonry. The Abbé Barruel in France and Professor Robison in Scotland both attacked continental Freemasonry (although Robison was himself a Mason and Barruel had been initiated after a fashion) in books that gained a wide circulation. Both Barruel's *Mémoires pour servir à l'histoire du jacobinisme* (1797) and Robison's *Proofs of a conspiracy* (also 1797) are at the same time mines of information and models of irrationality, giving to anti-Masons a host of hysterical denunciations and a great mass of supporting 'evidence' (albeit mostly to do with the Illuminati). Political fears also led to other attacks on Masonry. Banned briefly in Russia from 1797 to 1803, the Craft was finally and rigidly suppressed in 1826. While permitted in most other European countries, the unceasing religious opposition and unjust political repression that the Craft faced led some Freemasons to turn to anti-clerical activities and revolutionary political pursuits. This was, of course, quite contrary to the tenets of Freemasonry but, in the circumstances, not surprising; the inevitable clash between Church and Craft in post-Napoleonic Europe was to bring, however, little benefit to the Craft and little comfort to the Church.

3
Colonial Freemasonry

THE spread and development of British Freemasonry outside Europe mirrors the expansion of the British Empire. Wherever explorers, settlers, merchants, the military, or the navy went Freemasonry went with them or followed quickly afterwards. This raises the question of why Freemasonry should have been so popular in out of the way places. Obviously there was the appeal of its basic principles. Involvement with Freemasonry provided a link, however tenuous, with the old countries. But above all, in isolated areas where, in European terms, there was little civilization Freemasonry formed a social bond in emerging communities. In many places Freemasonry provided the only social life for the men in settlements, army stations, and new towns. When a lodge room or Masonic Hall was built it often became the social focal point of the community, being lodge room, public meeting hall, dance hall, and sometimes schoolroom. Even more than in the home countries the conviviality and fraternalism of Freemasonry were important in the lives of colonial brethren.

Freemasonry arrived in the colonies in four ways. There is no doubt that in some areas *time immemorial* lodges emerged—that is, lodges started at some unknown date by groups of men who had become Freemasons in the British isles and who met without any authority from a Grand Lodge or a Provincial Grand Master. Benjamin Franklin (Fig. 62) is believed to have been made a Mason in just such a self-constituted lodge in Philadelphia in 1731. The Antients Grand Lodge in England and the Grand Lodge of Ireland warranted many travelling lodges in army regiments, the lodges being able to meet wherever the regiment was stationed. These lodges could be formed only with the permission of the colonel of the regiment and were limited to drawing their candidates from the regiment. In many cases, however, they took in local citizens and the merchants and tradesmen who serviced the regiment. When the regiment moved on, the civilians who had joined it either applied to a local Masonic authority, if one existed, or to one of the home Grand Lodges for a warrant as a stationary lodge. This latter method was also applied by merchants and settlers who had become Freemasons before arriving in one of the new territories. Once a sufficient number appeared in a new community they would apply to one of the home Grand Lodges for authority to meet at a lodge. By far the most successful way to stimulate Masonic growth in the new colonies was to appoint a Provincial Grand Master, which the premier Grand Lodge and Grand Lodge of Scotland did to great advantage throughout the eighteenth century. Because of the distance from London and lack of efficient means of communication Provincial Grand Masters

61
Hippolito Joseph da Costa suffered at the hands of the Portuguese Inquisition but escaped to England in 1805 where he became an important member of the Duke of Sussex's Masonic circle.

62
Benjamin Franklin. Inventor,
publisher, diplomat and
patriot. A member of Lodges in
New England and Paris.

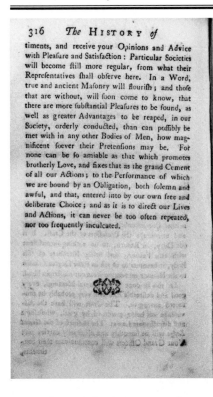

63
Boston was an early and important centre of Freemasonry in the American colonies.

were given authority to constitute new lodges. Such constitutions were supposed to be reported to the home Grand Lodges but the new lodges often went out of existence before this could happen. The Antients Grand Lodge in England actually warranted Provincial Grand Lodges which had the right to elect successive Provincial Grand Masters and to constitute new lodges. The most prolific of these was the Antients Provincial Grand Lodge of Nova Scotia which between 1780 and 1824 constituted nearly fifty lodges in Nova Scotia, New Brunswick, and other parts of Canada.

The prospect of wealth from plantations and the growing slave trade led to an early colonization of the islands of the Caribbean and West Indies, Freemasonry arriving with the settlers. English Provincial Grand Masters were appointed for Montserrat (1734), Leeward Islands (1737), Barbados (1740), Jamaica (1742), Bermuda (1744), Antigua (1754), Bahamas (1759), and the Grenadines (1764). In a number of cases the Province did not outlast the residence of the Provincial Grand Master but Barbados and Jamaica were to be great successes, each having a long succession of active Provincial Grand Masters and lodges. The area was also colonized by the French who, as the century progressed, introduced the various additional and high degree systems evolving in Europe. Indeed it was through the French introducing the Rite of Perfection into the West Indies, by giving a roving patent to Stephen Morin, that the Rite was developed, taken over

64 Right
Certificate issued by King Solomon Lodge No. 7, New York, to John Ledsam, 9 July 1767.

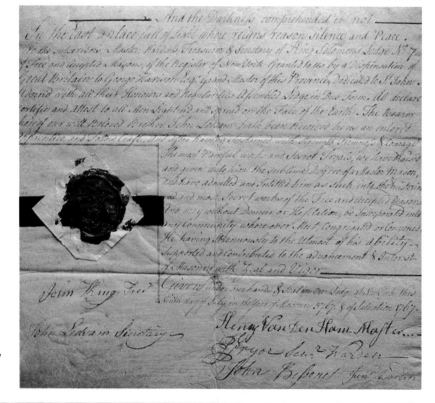

65 Below
Warrant for a travelling lodge in the Regiment of Loyal Surrey Rangers at Halifax, Nova Scotia, 5 February 1801.

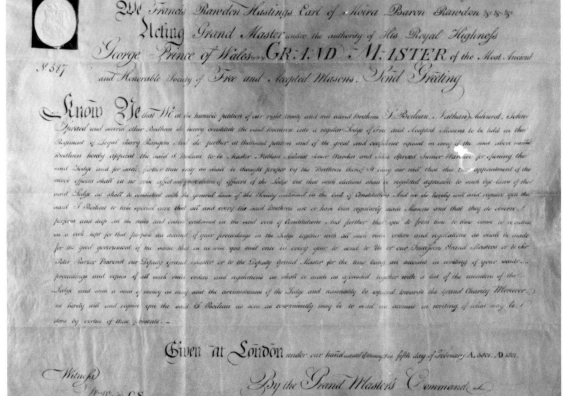

[6?]

DAYS *for choosing* CHURCH-WARDENS *and* VESTRY-MEN.

Kingston.	*St. Thomas in the East.*	*St. James.*
2d Thursday in Jan.	3d Monday in Jan.	2d Tuesday in Feb.
St. Catherine.	*St. George.*	*Trelawny.*
2d Tuesday in Jan.	2d Wednesd. in Jan.	2d Thursday in Feb.
Port-Royal.	*Westmoreland.*	
2d Wednesd. in Jan.	2d Tuesday in Jan.	*St. John.*
St. Andrew.	*St. Elizabeth.*	3d Thursday in Jan.
2d Friday in Jan.	2d Tuesday in Jan.	*St. Thomas in the Vale.*
Vere.	*St. Dorothy.*	1st Tuesday in Feb.
1st Wednesd. in Jan.	3d Wednesd. in Jan.	*Portland.*
Clarendon.	*St. Ann.*	2d Tuesday in March
1st Tuesday in Jan.	3d Friday in Jan.	
St. David.	*Hanover.*	*St. Mary.*
2d Saturday in Jan.	3d Tuesday in Feb.	2d Thursd. in March

DAYS *on which no Business is done at the* CUSTOM-HOUSE.

Queen's birth-day kept	Jan. 18.	Whitsun Tuesday	June 2.
King Charles I. mart.	30.	King's birth-day	4.
Shrove Tuesday	Feb. 24.	Fast	7.
Ash Wednesday	25.	Midsummer-day, and	
St. David	March 1	St. John Baptist.	24.
St. Patrick's	17.	Pr. of Wales' birth-day	Aug. 12.
Lady-day	25	Fast	28.
Good Friday	April 9	K. Geo. III. crowned	Sept. 22.
Easter Monday	12.	Michaelmas-day	29.
——— Tuesday	13	K. Geo. III. procl.	Oct. 26.
St. George	23	Gun-Powder Plot	Nov. 5.
King Charles II. rest.	May 29	St. Andrew	30.
Whitsun Monday	June 1	Christm. *and 3 days after*	Dec. 25.

LIST OF MASON LODGES IN JAMAICA, and their stated Meetings.

MOTHER LODGE, Nº I. held at Free-Masons Hall, Kingston, the *first* and *third* Saturday evenings in every month.

KINGSTON LODGE, Nº II. held at Allen's tavern, Kingston, the *first* and *third* Wednesday evenings in every month.

HARMONY LODGE, Nº III. HANOVER LODGE, at Lucea.

AMITY LODGE, held at Free-Masons Hall, Kingston, the *first* and *third* Tuesday evenings in every month.

ST. JAMES'S LODGE, Nº I. (*Ancient Masons*) held in Free-Masons Hall, Kingston, the *second* Saturday in every month.

ST. JAMES'S LODGE, Nº IV. held at Montego-Bay the *first* and *third* Monday Evenings of every month.

UNION LODGE, Nº V. held at Free-Masons Hall, Montego Bay, the *first* and *third* Saturday evenings in every month.

ST. ANDREWS LODGE, held at Halfway-Tree the Sunday evening nearest every full moon, whether before or after it.

SEVILLE LODGE, held at Laughlands the *first* Saturday in every month. ST. MARY'S Lodge, held in the parish of St. Mary

HANOVER LODGE, at Lucea. UNION LODGE, Sav. la Mar.

T

66

List of lodges in Jamaica from Douglass and Aikman's Almanack and Register for the Island of Jamaica, 1784.

THE

FREE-MASON'S GUIDE,

INTENDED

FOR THE

USE OF THE BRETHREN

𝕴𝖓 𝕴𝖓𝖉𝖎𝖆,

SELECTED

FROM

APPROVED WORKS

ON

THE ROYAL ART.

PRINTED BY R. W. WALKER,—TELEGRAPH PRESS,

1812.

67
Title page from an early handbook for Freemasons in India.

London 10th March 1789.

The Honble Society of Free Masons

to Thos Colcomb.

To a Free Masons Appron richley Embroidered in Gold Silver & Stone on white Leather Lined with blew Sattin and Trimd with rich Gold fringe and bullion with strings and Tossells &c &c ——— £28.. 0.. 0..

68 Above
Bill for the special apron and Constitutions for Omdat-al-Omrah, Nabob of the Camaric, initiated 1775.

69 Left
James Burnes was a Scottish Freemason who did much to promote both Freemasonry and education in India.

to the American states, and turned into the Ancient and Accepted Scottish Rite. Central to this development was Harry Andrew Francken, a Dutchman who settled in Kingston, Jamaica, and became a naturalized British subject to enable him, of all reasons, to become a Customs and Excise officer. Francken assiduously copied the regulations, rituals, and Morin's patent to promote the Rite; at least five of his bulky manuscripts are known to have survived, and he was instrumental in taking the Rite to the United States. The early history of the Scottish Rite is difficult to trace but it is more than possible that the transformation of the twenty-five degree Rite of Perfection into the thirty-three degree Ancient and Accepted Scottish Rite took place in the West Indies.

Freemasonry came to India in 1728 when an English lodge was set up in Fort William, now Calcutta (Figs. 62-3). The event was of sufficient importance for the petition to be recorded in the Grand Lodge Minutes. In 1729 two English Provincial Grand Masters were appointed—Captain Ralph Farwinter (sometimes spelt Farr Winter) for 'East India in Bengal' and James Dawson 'for East India'. In Madras it was the rival Antients Grand Lodge of England that held sway. Although the original Grand Lodge had appointed a Provincial Grand Master for Madras in 1767 (Captain Edmund Pascall) in 1768 the Antients established a Military Lodge at Fort St George which became the principal lodge on the Coast of Coromandel and acted as a Provincial Grand Lodge by warranting new lodges, establishing a charity fund, and building a Masonic Hall. Throughout the eighteenth century Freemasonry in India was in a constant state of flux.

The English had been joined by the Irish and Scots and occasionally the French made incursions, until they were finally driven out of the sub-continent. The constant movement of military units, the mobility of East India Company staff, and the various wars against Indian rulers meant that stability was hard to achieve. Lodges would be set up only to find that in a couple of years most of their members had been moved to other stations or had left India altogether. It was not until India was totally under British rule that stability was achieved.

The introduction of Freemasonry into India, and later the Far East, raised the questions of race and religion, which should have had no place in Freemasonry. The earliest extant record of a non-European being admitted into a lodge in India is that of Omdat-ul-Omrah, the Nabobs of the Carnatic, who was initiated in 1775. When the news reached the Grand Lodge of England they immediately agreed to send him 'a Masonic apron, elegantly decorated, and a *Book of Constitutions* bound in a most superb manner' at a cost of £37 17s 6d, (something over £500). Regrettably, the Nabobs did not prove to be a good Freemason in either his attendance or his conduct. As overseas lodges at this period did not

70 **Opposite**
Sir Herbert Abingdon Draper Compton 1770-1846. Provincial Grand Master for Madras 1812-14 and 1826-40. Watercolour.

send lists of members to their parent Grand Lodge it is impossible to say how many Indians entered Freemasonry, especially as local lodge records often fell foul of climate or insects. It would appear that it was not only the nineteenth century that Indians joined the Craft in any number. In some areas they were welcomed, but in others there was a distinct, and very unmasonic, hostility. With Parsees, Sikhs, and Zoroastrians there was little problem on religious grounds: they could all affirm a belief in a Supreme Being. With Hindus there were considerable problems. The belief that Hindus worshipped many gods and that Hinduism was a way of life rather than a religious belief caused many lodges to reject Hindus on the grounds that they could not fulfil the essential qualifications of belief in a Supreme Being (see p. 117). The caste system was also a problem initially, but as the nineteenth century progressed so caste began to disappear within the lodge room, whatever the conditions outside. Similarly, although religious differences were a problem in Indian society

71
Henry Price, 1697-1780.
Appointed Provincial Grand
Master for New England in
1733. A year later his
jurisdiction was extended to all
of North America.

they were forgotten in lodge and many Indian lodges did indeed become, in the words of the Ancient Charge, 'the happy means of conciliating friendship among those who must otherwise have remained at a perpetual distance'.

There are many stories, now beyond proof, that Freemasonry entered North America with the earliest colonists, long before the formation of the original Grand Lodge in England in 1717.

There is certainly circumstantial evidence that self-constituted lodges appeared in parts of the American colonies, notably Boston and Philadelphia, by 1730. What is certain is that the Grand Lodge of England stimulated the growth of Freemasonry by the early appointment of Provincial Grand Masters who were no mere figureheads but very active in promoting the Craft. The first appointment, on 5 June 1730, was David Cox, whose territory was New York, New Jersey, and Pennsylvania. He was followed, on 13 April 1733, by Henry Price (Fig. 71), who was given the vaguer territory of New England, over which he ruled intermittently from 1733 to 1768. The succession of English Provincial Grand Masters was as follows:

New England
1733   Henry Price
1736   Robert Tomlinson

Georgia
1735   Robert Hugh Lacy
1760   Grey Elliott
1773   Hon. Noble Jones

South Carolina
1736   John Hammerton
1754   Peter Leigh
1770   Sir Egerton Leigh
1788   John Deas

New York
1737   Richard Riggs
1751   Francis Goelct
1753   George Harrison
1767   Sir John Johnston

North America
1743   Thomas Oxenard
1755   Jeremy Gridley
1768   Joseph Rowe

Pennsylvania
1749   William Allen

Carolina
1761   Benjamin Smith

Virginia
1766   Hon. Presley Thornton

1773   Peyton Randolph
North Carolina
1771   Joseph Montfort
Allied Nations in North America
1791   William Augustus Bowles

Not to be outdone, the English Antients Grand Lodge warranted Provincial Grand Lodges in New York and Pennsylvania and the Irish and Scots were equally active. By the outbreak of the War of Independence there were about a hundred lodges in the British colonies and some French Masonic units in Louisiana.

Amongst the earliest of the notable American Freemasons was Benjamin Franklin. Initiated into a self-constituted Philadelphian Lodge in 1731, he did much to publicize the existence of Freemasonry by reporting on local meetings in the press and reproducing Masonic items from the British press. In 1734 he printed an American edition of Anderson's 1723 *Constitutions*, the first Masonic book published in America and now one of the rarest Masonic publications (Fig. 72). He became much involved in Freemasonry in Pennsylvania, including assisting in laying the foundation stone of the first Masonic building in America, the Masonic Hall in Philadelphia, on 24 June 1755. Spending most of the last thirty-three years of his life in the British Isles and France, he joined the Nine Sisters Lodge in Paris in 1778, having taken part in the initiation of Voltaire on 7 April 1788, was its Master and a member of two other French lodges.

With good intentions many American Masonic historians in the past have made too much of the part played by Freemasonry in the War of Independence, giving birth to the conspiracy theory that the American Revolution was inspired by Freemasonry, planned in Masonic lodges, and carried out by Masonic leaders. Their extravagant writing and oratory was taken up by Bernard Fay in his *Revolution and Freemasonry*, of which various editions and translations were published in the 1930s, and turned against them for Fay was in the pockets of the notoriously anti-Masonic General von Ludendorff and Adolf Hitler, who used Fay's book as propaganda in their anti-semitic and anti-Masonic machinations. The plain truth is that in the American Revolution there were prominent Freemasons on both sides and no evidence has been found to substantiate the claim that the Revolution was hatched in any of the lodges; indeed there is a great deal of evidence to show that members of what ultimately became opposing factions were, before the outbreak of hostilities, members of the same lodges. Modern American Masonic historians, in preparation for the bicentennial of the United States, carried out a great deal of research into the revolutionary period and junked many cherished

THE
CONSTITUTIONS
OF THE
FREE-MASONS.

CONTAINING THE

History, Charges, Regulations, &c.
of that moſt Ancient and Right
Worſhipful FRATERNITY.

For the Uſe of the LODGES.

LONDON Printed; *Anno* 5723.
Re-printed in *Philadelphia* by ſpecial Order, for the Uſe
of the Brethren in *NORTH-AMERICA.*
In the Year of Maſonry 5734, *Anno Domini* 1734.

72
Franklin's American edition of the 1723 Constitutions, the first Masonic book published in America. Only 18 copies are now known. This example was the property of Henry Price.

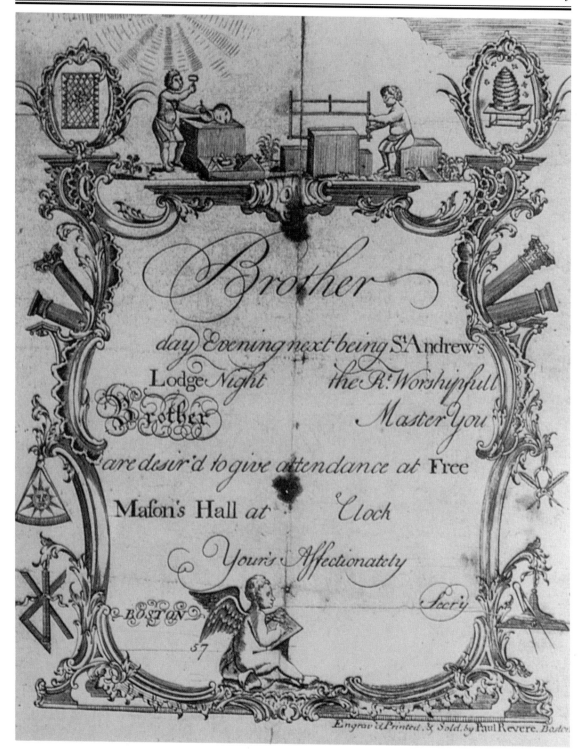

legends. Of the seven Provincial Grand Masters in office at the outbreak of hostilities, five were supporters of the king and government. Only eight of those who signed the Declaration of Independence, out of a total of fifty-six, can be positively identified as Freemasons. Of the fifty-five delegates who attended the Constitutional Convention in 1787, at which the Constitution was agreed and signed, nine were definitely Freemasons, five were later to become Freemasons, twenty-two were certainly not Freemasons, and thirteen have been *claimed* as Freemasons on very slight and unsubstantiated evidence.

Patriotic fervour apart, what has clouded many minds is the fact that a number of prominent and popular heroes of the American Revolution were Freemasons. Paul Revere (Fig. 73), Benjamin Franklin, John Paul Jones, General Andrew Jackson, the Marquis de Lafayette (Fig. 74), James Monroe (later president), and, of course, George Washington (Fig. 75).

The combination of Washington as a Mason, revolutionary leader, and first President has proved too much for some commentators and the importance of Washington as a Freemason has been overstressed. he was initiated in the Fredericksburg Lodge, Virginia, in 1752, was later Master of Alexandria Lodge No. 22, Virginia, in 1788, but refused the Grand Mastership of Virginia in 1777 and again refused nomination as Grand Master of a proposed General Grand Lodge for the United States, a project that was never realized. Examination of contemporary records show Washington to have been an enthusiastic Freemason but fairly inactive, which is not a criticism and hardly surprising considering the pressure on him, first, as leading general of the revolutionary army and, second, as the first head of State of a new country. Commenting on his membership of Freemasonry in a letter of 1798 Washington stated: 'So far as I am acquainted with the doctrines and principles of Freemasonry, I conceive them to be founded in beneficence, and to be exercised only for the good of mankind. I cannot, therefore, upon this ground with-hold my approbation from it.'

Once the American colonies had won their independence and the United States had come into being the hundred or so lodges in the former colonies gradually and silently withdrew their allegiances from the British Grand Lodges and began to form their own governing bodies. The transition was not always smooth and in some States rivals were formed, but gradually one Grand Lodge appeared in each of the States. In 1778 moves were made to form a single Grand Lodge to cover the whole of the new United States and a petition was addressed to all of the Provincial Grand Masters. In 1780 the Grand Lodge of Pennsylvania proceeded not only to agree to the proposition but to elect, without his knowledge, George Washington as Grand Master. The project was stillborn and the

73 Opposite
Paul Revere, in addition to his ride, was noted as a silversmith and engraver. He produced Masonic jewels and engraved plates for certificates, such as this one for St Andrew's Lodge, Boston.

The Marquis de Lafayette became involved in American Freemasonry during the period of the Revolutionary War.

75
George Washington in his regalia. Anonymous oil portrait.

76 Far left
Edward, Duke of Kent, 1767-1820, was appointed Provincial Grand Master for Lower Canada by the Antients Grand Lodge and greatly revived Freemasonry in the Province.

77 Above
The funeral of Sir John Johnson, English Provincial Grand Master for New York 1771-5 and for Canada 1788-1830. Mural in the Grand Lodge building at Montreal.

78 Left
The election of a Provincial Grand Master by Military lodges within Wolfe's army at Quebec, 1759. Mural at Montreal.

National Grand Lodge never came into being. As new States were added to the Union they formed State Grand Lodges and any subsequent attempt to form a national or federal Grand Lodge has always been met by strenuous objections. The former colonial lodges did not inform the home Grand Lodges of their independence and many of them were continued on the registers of the British Grand Lodges until the early nineteenth century when it became all too apparent that they had changed their allegiances.

British Freemasonry had been taken into Canada at an early stage in Nova Scotia and New Brunswick and French Freemasonry into Quebec (Fig. 76). The area that is now Ontario was less easy to settle and Freemasonry did not easily establish itself. Difficulties of transport and communication apart, there were local rivalries which were less than helpful. HRH Edward, Duke of Kent was appointed to a military command in Lower Canada and the Antients Grand Lodge of England appointed him their Provincial Grand Master for that area, despite his being an honorary Past Grand Master of the rival premier Grand Lodge. His arrival in Canada did much to revitalize Freemasonry and the Provincial Grand Lodge flourished. The French had been chased out of Quebec and an English Province was established. In the eighteenth century the premier Grand Lodge of England had Provinces in Canada as follows:

Cape Breton and Louisberg
1746   Capt. Robert Cummins
Nova Scotia
1757   Major Erasmus J. Phillips
1760   Hon. Jonathan Bakker
Canada
1760   Col. Hon. Simon Frazier
1764   Milbourne West
1788   Sir John Johnston Bt.
Quebec
1767   Hon. John Collins
1786   Col. Christopher Carleton
Upper Canada
1792   William Jarvis

4

The Union in England

ON 27 December 1813 a great celebration was held at Freemasons' Hall, London, when the Premier and Antients Grand Lodges formally joined together to form the United Grand Lodge of England. The road to union had not been an easy one. In 1810 committees had been appointed by both Grand Lodges to negotiate an equable union. That appointed by the Premier Grand Lodge had full negotiating rights, but the Antients, democratic to the end, insisted that its committee report back after each meeting and that its report be debated in full by the whole Grand Lodge. After two years of toing and froing, with nothing being resolved, the Premier Grand Lodge, not unnaturally, became impatient and called in the support of their Acting Grand Master, Francis Rawdon, 2nd Earl of Moira (Fig. 79). His lordship rather testily wrote to the Antients Grand Lodge in June 1811, stating that unless their committee was given authority to negotiate without every dot and comma being confirmed he could see no point in continuing discussions. His bluntness paid off and the Antients Committee was given the authority required, but discussions still dragged on.

Significant changes at the head of both Grand Lodges brought matters to a head in 1813. The Prince of Wales, who had been Grand Master of the Premier Grand Lodge since 1790, became Prince Regent (Fig. 80). Moira, who had been his chief Masonic advisor, was posted abroad to become Governor and Commander-in-Chief of Bengal. The Prince of Wales felt that he could not carry on as Grand Master without his trusted advisor. Additionally, it was felt in Court circles that a monarch, or his regent, should not be subject to an annual election, in any organization, that he could conceivably lose. The Prince resigned and his younger

79 **Far left**
*Francis, 2nd Earl of Moira
(later 1st Marquess of
Hastings), Acting Grand Master
of the premier Grand Lodge
1790-1813.*

80
*George, Prince of Wales (later
George IV). Grand Master of
the premier Grand Lodge
1790-1813. Portrait by Sir
Thomas Lawrence.*

brother HRH Augustus Frederick, Duke of Sussex[2] was elected Grand Master on 7 April 1813. John, 4th Duke of Athol,[3] who had begun his second term as Grand Master of the Antients in 1791, announced his resignation on 8 November 1813. Yet another of the sons of King George III was pressed into service. HRH Edward, Duke of Kent,[4] the father of Queen Victoria, had been a member of both Grand Lodges and accepted, with alacrity, nomination as Grand Master of the Antients. He was installed on 1 December 1813. It says much for the authority of princes in those days that within less than two months of the royal brothers becoming Grand Masters of the opposing parties they had not only sorted out the differences but had persuaded both Grand Lodges to ratify the Articles of Union and arranged the great ceremonial which brought the United Grand Lodge into being on 27 December 1813.

The first problem brought about by the Union, the Grand Mastership, was easily settled by the Duke of Kent standing down and nominating his brother, Sussex (Fig. 81). A wiser choice could not have been made. Sussex was a young man, well liked by society in general, and had both the ability and the position to put through the necessary changes to ensure that the union was maintained. With hindsight it would appear that the Duke of Sussex had four main intentions: to assert Grand Lodge's authority over all the lodges of the two former obediences; to standardize; to complete the de-Christianization of the Craft and Royal Arch; and to maintain the Craft's superiority over any other Masonic order.

The assertion of Grand Lodge's authority was immediate. The lodges under both former Grand Lodges gave allegiance to the United Grand Lodge; had they not, although no threat had been made, they would have lost their authority to meet. Recognition by the Grand Lodges of Ireland and Scotland had been assured by keeping both informed at all stages and inviting them to be represented at the union celebrations. Since the union, only once has the Grand Lodge's authority been challenged. In 1819 a number of Liverpool lodges refused to come to terms with the changes brought about by the union and the United Grand Lodge was forced into a situation in which it would only safeguard its authority by erasing the lodges from the register. The lodges immediately formed themselves into a Grand Lodge, which became centred on Wigan and is now known as the Wigan Grand Lodge. It was never a particularly successful body and ceased meeting in 1833. One lodge, however, Sincerity, meeting in Wigan, continued as an independent lodge until 1913 when it petitioned to be regularized and became No. 3677 on the register.

Standardization began immediately. The Articles of Union provided for the warranting of a special Lodge of Reconciliation whose brief was to reconcile the two former ritual systems and bring about a standard form of ritual to be adopted by all English lodges. To a certain extent the Lodge

81 **Opposite**
Augustus Frederick, Duke of Sussex. Grand Master of the premier Grand Lodge 1813 and of the United Grand Lodge 1813-43.

of Reconciliation over-reacted to its brief. It not only reconciled the two systems but redesigned the ceremonies. Before the union the actual ceremonies had been fairly brief and much of the explanation of the principles, tenets, and symbolism had been done in the form of catechetical lectures. Similarly, there had been very little difference between the meeting itself and the social conviviality enjoyed by the brethren. The Lodge of Reconciliation greatly extended the ceremonies by inclusion of material from the lectures which had gradually dropped out of use. This led to a natural break between lodge business and conviviality and the necessity of having separate lodge and supper rooms, leading to the development of lodge rooms and Masonic Halls to replace meetings in inns and taverns. These changes also brought about a fundamental shift in emphasis. For much of the eighteenth century English Freemasonry had been largely a convivial society; the revisions by the Lodge of Reconciliation placed the emphasis firmly on the ritual aspect and the Masonic principles of morality and brotherhood.

As promulgation of the revised ritual was by demonstration and word of mouth, and because the Grand Lodge would not permit printed or manuscript versions to be circulated, the aim of every lodge working a standardized ritual was not achieved. Whilst English lodges follow the

82-84
Three of a set of seven print depicting Craft ceremonies engraved by Thomas Palser 1809-12, based on a German series printed 1745. Palser simply updated the costume.

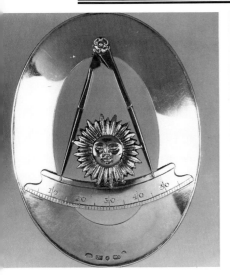

85 Above
Jewel of George Woodcock as
Grand Master of the Grand
Lodge of Wigan 18??.

86 Above right
The Masonic Hall, Bath,
dedicated by the Duke of Sussex
1819.

87 Right
Standard designs for lodge
officers' jewels introduced in
1814.

1st row: Senior Warden,
Master, Junior Warden
2nd row: Chaplain, Treasurer,
Secretary, Director of
Ceremonies, Deacons
3rd row: Charity Steward,
Almoner, ADC, Organist,
Assistant Secretary
4th row: Inner Guard,
Stewards, Tyler.

same basic principles of ritual and format of ceremonies there remain wide variations in the details of wording and ceremonial.

The earliest visible form of standardization was in regalia. Before the union, members were at liberty to design their own aprons and jewels, as Masonic medals are termed. Rules were laid down for the aprons and jewels of Grand Officers and the principal officers of a lodge (Figs. 87-8), but examples survive of beautifully hand-made members' aprons decorated with a multiplicity of Masonic emblems, either hand-painted or embroidered. Similarly, a wealth of gold, silver-gilt, silver, and enamelled jewels, masterpieces of the jeweller's art, have survived. In March 1814 the Board of Works presented to Grand Lodge designs for standardized aprons for the various grades of member and standard patterns for jewels for Grand, Provincial, and Lodge officers. Since then, the only latitude for individuality that has been allowed is in designs for Founders' and Past Masters' jewels of individual lodges.

88
A collection of 19th century English presentation jewels, awarded for particular services to a lodge.

89
An unknown Senior Warden in
the regalia adopted in 1814.
Unsigned watercolour, c.1840.

90
*Philip Broadfoot. One of a
group of peripatetic ritual
teachers who demonstrated the
revised ritual of 1816. In his
Royal Arch regalia.*

In its early organized state English Freemasonry had been Christian in the sense that Christianity, indeed Anglicanism, was the only recognized religion in England. There were Christian references in the rituals; for example, St John the Baptist and St John the Evangelist were referred to as the patron saints of Freemasonry and the half-yearly installations of lodge officers usually took place on their days in June and December. The rituals did not refer specifically to Jesus Christ, but some of the symbolism could be given a Trinitarian gloss. From the mid-1720s Jews began to appear in lodge membership lists and as the century progressed the overt Christian references and symbolism began to disappear from the ritual and lectures. The Duke of Sussex was a man of great tolerance in matters of religion in a very intolerant period. A supporter of Catholic Emancipation, a Hebrew scholar who publicly associated himself with Jews and involved himself in Jewish learned societies and charitable organizations, Sussex was a firm believer that Freemasonry should be, as it was intended, open to all men who believed in a Supreme Being, regardless of how they

91
Thomas Dunckerley 1724-95. A
natural son of George II, he
was Provincial Grand Master of
eight Provinces, Grand
Superintendent in 18 Royal
Arch Provinces and a great
promoter of Freemasonry.

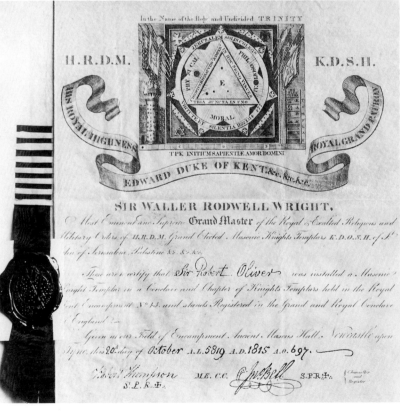

92
Engraved Knights Templar
certificate designed by
Dunckerley when the Grand
Conclave was formed in 1790.

expressed that belief. To this end he oversaw the completion of the de-Christianizing of the Craft. Similarly, when his attention was turned to the Royal Arch (which originally had been intensely Christian but which, like the Craft, had gradually been losing its overtly Christian elements) the Royal Arch itself, as the completion of the third degree, was made universal by the removal of any Christian reference.

The Duke of Sussex has often been accused of preventing the continuance and growth of the additional degree and orders in England. This is an unjust criticism. He did, however, use his position to keep these other branches of Freemasonry as far in the background as possible, but this was done with the best of motives. His main concern was that the union of the two Grand Lodges should succeed and the situation of rival Grand Lodges should never be returned to. He saw the additional degrees as a possible distraction from his main course and as a probable course of argument which could lead to dissension in Grand Lodge, as was to happen in 1856 when attempts were made to have the Mark degree recognized as part of 'pure antient Freemasonry'.

The great explosion of additional degrees in eighteenth-century Europe had little effect in the British Isles. Elements of the Mark degree began to appear in the 1750s. In 1791 Thomas Dunckerley (Fig. 91) set up a Grand Conclave of Knights Templar and in the same decade evidence for the Rose Croix degree (now the 18th degree of the Ancient and Accepted Rite) began to appear. Lodges under the Antients Grand Lodge had worked the Mark and other degrees as preliminaries to the Royal Arch, but the more arcane philosophical, hermetic, cabbalistic, and alchemical degrees, many of which are best described as quasi-Maosnic and which flourished in France and Germany, found no adherents in the British Isles.

The Duke of Sussex did not prevent the working of additional degrees but he secured control of governing bodies for them and effectively 'sat' on them until the union had succeeded and the authority of the Grand Lodge as the supreme Masonic authority was established. Shortly after his death there was a resurgence of interest and governing bodies were brought into being. J.C. Burckhardt had been the duke's Deputy Grand Master in the Knights Templar, but the Grand Conclave had not met since 1812. It was revived in 1843, gradually re-established its authority over existing Conclaves and brought new ones, at home and abroad, into being (Fig. 92). The Great Priory, as it is now called, controls the degrees of Knight Templar and Knight of Malta and has 532 preceptories under its control.

In 1819 the Duke of Sussex, with the Duke of Leinster (Grand Master of Ireland 1813-74) acquired a patent from the Supreme Council of France enabling him to set up a Supreme Council 33° for the British Isles. It was never acted upon. In 1845 the Revd Dr George Oliver (Fig. 93) and Dr

93 Right
Rev Dr George Oliver
1782-1867. The most prolific of
English Masonic authors with a
reputation that brought him
Masonic honours from China,
Australasia, America and
Europe.

94 Below
Dr Robert Crucefix in his
regalia as Past Junior Grand
Deacon. Remembered today as
the originator of the Asylum for
Aged and Decayed Freemasons,
now the Royal Masonic
Benevolent Institution.

95 Far right
Mark certificate issued to J.A.F.
Albuqurque, Plymouth, 13
February 1829. The earliest
known Mark certificate.

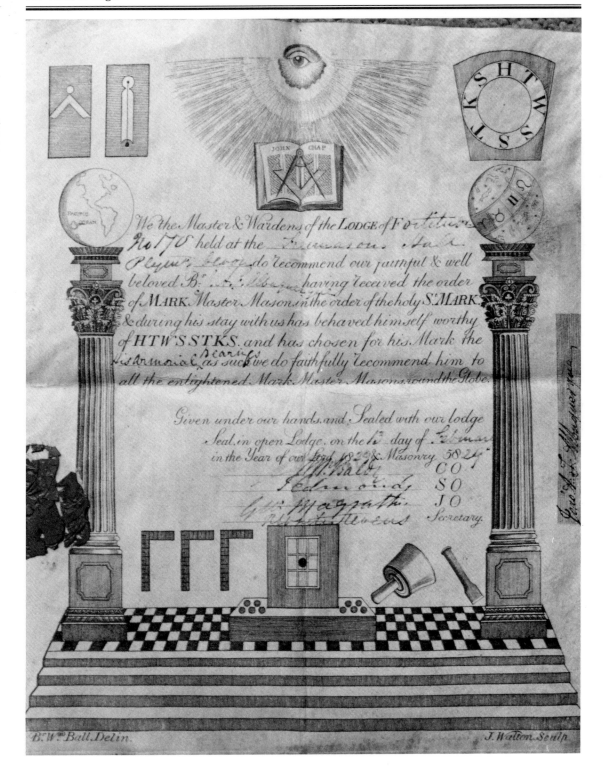

96 **Above**
Major Francis Irwin of Bristol.
A retired Sapper with a
military sinecure, he was one of
a group who between 1860 and
1890 'revived' or invented
numerous fringe Masonic
Orders.

97 **Above right**
Dr William Wynn Westcott
1848-1925. A Coroner,
enthusiastic Freemason and
dabbler in arcane studies, he
was Supreme Magus of the
Societas Rosicrucian in Anglia.

Robert Crucifix (Fig. 94), amongst others, received a patent from the Supreme Council for the Northern Jurisdiction of the USA which appointed them to the 33rd degree and enabled them to set up a Supreme Council of the Ancient and Accepted Rite for England. It was introduced into England as a purely Christian order, which it still remains, and only the 18th and 30th-33rd degrees are worked in full. As the Rose Croix degree had originally been worked in Conclaves of Knights Templar it was initially difficult for the Supreme Council to assert its authority over the degree until a compact was signed with the Knights Templar authorities in 1871, since when the Supreme Council has had undisputed control over all its degrees.

The revival of the Mark degree caused something of a storm within the Grand Lodge and generated a great deal of rancorous correspondence in the Masonic press of the day. Until 1856 the Mark ritual, which deals with an incident in the building of King Solomon's Temple, had no governing body. In that year an attempt, at first successful, was made to gain Grand Lodge's agreement to the Mark being recognized as part of the Craft and

98
John Yarker 1833-1913. The doyen of fringe Masonic activity in England, he was head of the Ancient and Primitive Rite of Memphis and Misraim.

for it to be worked in lodges between the second and third degrees (Fig. 95). The motion was accepted but when put for confirmation at the next Grand Lodge was vigorously objected to by the Grand Registrar and other senior Grand Officers. They argued that pure, ancient Freemasonry having been defined, and accepted, in the union negotiations as consisting of the three Craft degrees together with the Royal Arch, Grand Lodge would not materially alter that declaration by now including the Mark in lodge work. An acrimonious argument followed and the earlier decision was reversed. The supporters of the Mark must have expected this result for within a few days of the motion being overturned a Grand Lodge of Mark Master Masons was set up, which now has 1418 lodges at home and abroad and since 1872 has had attached to it the Royal Ark mariner degree. This degree originated in the late eighteenth century and its ritual is based upon the story of Noah and his ark.

The second half of the nineteenth century in England was to see a proliferation of degrees and orders, many of which appear to have either existed only on paper or to have been worked by a handful of people and died with their originators. Predominant in the group who were largely responsible for much of this activity were Major Francis Irwin of Bristol (Fig. 96), Kenneth McKenzie, Robert Wentworth Little, and Dr W. Wynn Westcott (Fig. 97), all of London and John Yarker of Manchester (Fig. 98). Amongst all their hybrid activity, and that of others, a number of degrees and orders were revived, or reputedly revived, which still exist today. In 1865 R.W. Little 'revived' the Grand Imperial Conclave of the Red Cross of Constantine, which governs the degrees of Knight of the Red Cross of Constantine, Knight of the Holy Sepulchre, and Knight of St John the Evangelist. The following year, 1866, Little 'revived' the Societas Rosicruciana in Anglia. The Soc. Ros., as it is commonly known, is not a Masonic order but requires its members to be Master Masons and Christians. Divided into nine grades, its purpose is to study 'the revelation of philosophy, science and theosophy'. The Excellent and Super Excellent degrees that had been worked by the Antients Grand Lodge as part of their Royal Arch system were fully revived in 1873 when, by virtue of a warrant from New York, a Grand Council of Royal and Select Masters, referred to in shorthand as the cryptic degrees, was formed. There had been various attempts to set up a governing body to control a number of disparate degrees which were being worked in various parts of the country. Success came in 1879 when the Grand Council of the allied Masonic degrees was organized. It now controls five degrees: St Laurence the Martyr; Knight of Constantinople; Grand Tilers of King Solomon; Red Cross of Babylon; and Grand High Priest. Another degree it originally claimed control over was the Secret Monitor, based upon the biblical story of David and Jonathan, but in 1887 a Grand Council of the Order of the Secret Monitor was set up. In 1895 John Yarker revived the degree of Knight Templar Priest and a college was set up in Newcastle-upon-Tyne. The degree can be traced back to Ireland in the late eighteenth century and was popular in Lancashire in the early nineteenth century. The Newcastle college became the Grand College in 1925. The last major order to be instituted, in 1913, was the Worshipful Society of Free Masons, Rough Masons, Walkers, Slaters, Paviours, Plasterers, and Bricklayers, usually referred to as the Operatives. Working a seven-degree system, its original publicists claimed it as a revival of the ceremonies of the original operative stonemasons, a claim for which no evidence exists.

All of these degrees and orders are termed *additional* because they are in addition to, not replacements for, basic Freemasonry, which consists of the Craft and Royal Arch. All of them require candidates for membership to be at least a Master Mason. Although some of them have degrees numerically higher than the third degree, whilst others have high-sounding titles, they are in no way superior to the Craft. Nor are their governing bodies superior to the Grand Lodge, which is the supreme

Masonic governing body. The laboured argument by Stephen Knight in *The Brotherhood* that the Supreme Council of the Ancient and Accepted Rite was the real, secret governing body of English Freemasonry to which even the Grand Master was subservient was greeted with derision by members of the Rite. No decision taken by the Supreme Council can have any effect on the Craft. The members of the Supreme Council, as Craft Masons, owe allegiance to the Grand Lodge and the Grand Master, who is not a member of the Rite. On the contrary, the Ancient and Accepted Rite is dependent upon the Craft for its membership; were the Grand Lodge to take against it and ban its members from joining, the Rite would cease to exist as a regular Masonic body.

The additional degrees had a similarly haphazard development in Ireland and Scotland. In Ireland there is a much greater control and no

99
Robert Freke Gould 1836-1915. The lynch-pin of the authentic school of Masonic research his monolithic History and Antiquities of Freemasonry *(1882-7) is still a standard reference work.*

100

A typical example of a French certificate issued by lodges under the Grand Orient of France in the first half of the 19th century.

additional degree or order can meet without the permission of the Grand Lodge. The Mark and Excellent degrees are worked in Ireland as parts of the Royal Arch system. The Great Priory of Knights Templar used to claim an origin of 1770, but it is possible that British Knights Templary developed in Ireland. It was certainly exported from there to Scotland and may have come to England through Portsmouth or Bristol. Although the Duke of Leinster had been party to the grant of an Ancient and Accepted Rite patent to the Duke of Sussex in 1819 he either had a short memory or grew impatient with the Duke of Sussex's lack of action for in 1824 he accepted a patent from the Supreme Council for the Southern jurisdication of the USA (the 'mother' Supreme Council) from which the present Supreme Council of Ireland resulted. A problem arose because an equivalent of the Rose Croix was worked as the Prince Mason degree in Ireland. Happily, the two are now reconciled.

In Scotland the Mark can be worked both in the Craft or the Royal Arch and the Excellent is a preliminary to the latter. It was the Grand Chapter (Royal Arch) of Scotland's invading of English territory by warranting Mark Lodges in Lancashire that precipitated the Mark debate in England in 1856. The Knights Templar degree had a somewhat unhappy history of schisms, but reconciliation was achieved in 1909. The Ancient and Accepted Rite was introduced in 1846 by a patent from a French Supreme Council. Scotland is the home of the Royal Order of Scotland, the Grand Lodge of which was revived in 1839 and now has Provincial Grand Lodges throughout the world.

To return to the union in England, one of the beneficial effects was the development of the close contact and cooperation between the English, Irish, and Scottish Grand Lodges. In 1814 delegations from all three met together in London and agreed an International Compact. By this they recognized each other's sovereignty and agreed to regard home territory as closed to each other; areas outside the British Isles where no Grand Lodge existed became free territory in which all three could set up new lodges. This close cooperation, whilst not intervening in each other's affairs, has continued to the present day. As the three oldest Grand Lodges, and the lineal descendents of the originators of Freemasonry, the three British Grand Lodges are looked upon by the regular Grand Lodges as the guardians of Masonic regularity. Their close cooperation was to become increasingly important as new Grand Lodges emerged. Recognition by the three British Grand Lodges set the seal of regularity on any new Grand Lodge; failure to do so generally led to them being considered irregular by all recognized Grand Lodges.

Concern with regularity was to become a major issue in the mid-1870s. The history of Freemasonry in France is very complex; the myriad additional degree systems in which there was often schism, and the uncertainty about whether the Grand Orient of France was sovereign or under the partial control of a Supreme Council, only complicated matters further. There was also a growing feeling that the Grand Orient was rather more involved in politics and anti-clericalism than was proper for a Masonic body. A bombshell was dropped in 1877 when the Grand Orient resolved to remove all references to God from its *Constitutions* and rituals and removed the Bible from its lodges. At a stroke they had renounced one of the landmarks of Freemasonry: belief in a Supreme Being. Within a very short time the other regular Grand Lodges withdrew recognition from the Grand Orient of France, hoping that their actions would cause the French to reconsider and return to the three fundamental principles of Freemasonry. It was a vain hope. The Grand Orient was to stray even further from these principles and involved itself actively in politics, at times becoming almost a political party. Indeed it was probably due to the political and anti-clerical actions of the Grand Orient that the particularly

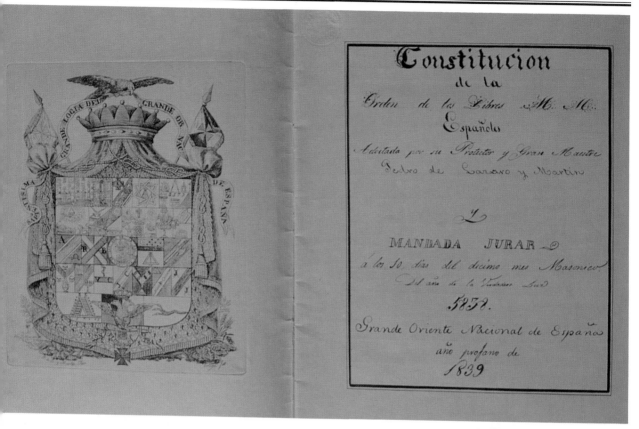

101
Armorial plate and title page of the MS Constitutions of the National Grand Orient of Spain, 1839.

rabid form of anti-Masonry developed in France.

The Grand Orient of France was not alone in its actions. Freemasonry had been largely stamped out in Spain and Portugal by both government decree and the activities of the Inquisition. Despite this, bodies regularly sprang up in both countries claiming to be Grand Lodges or Grand Orients. Not only were they all riven by internal strife but many were thinly disguised political groups. None of these were recognized by the body of regular Freemasonry. After the break with the Grand Orient of France the question of regularity gradually became a growing concern, the more so as new Grand Lodges began to develop. Over the years the United Grand Lodge of England had gradually evolved principles of recognition but they were not formally codified until 1929. After discussion they were adopted in Ireland and Scotland and became the standard on which other regular Grand Lodges based their recognitions. As they enshrine basic principles they are worth reproducing here:

The M.W. The Grand Master having expressed a desire that the Board would draw up a statement of the Basic Principles on which this Grand Lodge could be invited to recognize any Grand Lodge applying for recognition by the English Jurisdiction, the

Board of General Purposes has gladly complied. The result, as follows, has been approved by the Grand Master and it will form the basis of a questionnaire to be forwarded in future to each Jurisdiction requesting English recognition. The Board desires that not only such bodies but the Brethren generally throughout the Grand Master's Jurisdiction shall be fully informed as to those Basic Principles of Freemasonry for which the Grand Lodge of England has stood throughout its history.

1. Regularity of origin; i.e. each Grand Lodge shall have been established lawfully by a duly recognised Grand Lodge or by three or more regularly constituted Lodges.

2. That a belief in the G.A.O.T.U. and His revealed will shall be an essential qualification for membership.

3. That all Initiates shall take their Obligation on or in full view of the open Volume of the Sacred Law, by which is meant the revelation from above which is binding on the conscience of the particular individual who is being initiated.

4. That the membership of the Grand Lodge and individual Lodges shall be composed exclusively of men; and that each Grand Lodge shall have no Masonic intercourse of any kind with mixed Lodges or bodies which admit women to membership.

5. That the Grand Lodge shall have sovereign jurisdiction over the Lodges under its control; i.e. that it shall be a responsible, independent, self-governing organisation, with sole and undisputed authority over the Craft or Symbolic Degrees (Entered Apprentice, Fellow Craft, and Master Mason) within its Jurisdiction; and shall not in any way be subject to, or divide such authority with, a Supreme Council or other Power claiming any control or supervision over those degrees.

6. That the three Great Lights of Freemasonry (namely, the Volume of the Sacred Law, the Square, and the Compasses) shall always be exhibited when the Grand Lodge or its subordinate Lodges are at work, the chief of these being the Volume of the Sacred Law.

7. That the discussion of religion and politics within the Lodge shall be strictly prohibited.

8. That the principles of the Antient Landmarks, customs and usages of the Craft shall be strictly observed.

5
British
Freemasonry

*I*RELAND and Scotland did not escape the problems exper-
ienced by English Freemasonry. In 1801 one Alexander Seton had
been appointed Deputy Grand Secretary of Ireland. Vain, arrogant,
and money-grabbing, Seton's first action was to remove all the records
from the house of his predecessor. Having been refused the fees due to
the Deputy Grand Treasurer, Seton began pocketing some of the dues
being sent to the Grand Lodge by individual lodges and selling the dormant warrants of lodges that had gone out of existence. An anonymous
pamphlet war against the Grand Treasurer and his Deputy ensued,
particularly aimed at the Ulster lodges, which had separate grievances with
the Grand Lodge. Matters came to a head in 1806 when Seton was
dismissed, an action resulting in nearly two years of chaos with two groups
in Dublin claiming to be the legitimate Grand Lodge. Lord Donoughmore, the Grand Master, was forced to intervene in 1808. In 1807 the
Grand Lodge had expelled Seton, but Lord Donoughmore persuaded
both sides to agree that Seton would be reinstated provided that he return
all the records to the Grand Lodge. The return of recent records would,
of course, reveal Seton's chicanery. Not surprisingly, he refused to return
certain records and the revocation of his expulsion was rescinded.

Disaffected lodges in Ulster seized on the troubles in Dublin and, in
1808, members from 311 met at Dungannon and declared a Grand East
of Ulster with Col. W. Irvine as its Grand Master and Seton as Deputy
Grand Secretary. The new body got off to a bad start by electing Grand
Officers without their prior consent. Seton continued his financial
chicanery, to the extent that lodges were ordered to pay their dues and fees
to the Grand Treasurer and not to Seton. By 1810, thirty-seven of the

102
William 1st Duke of Leinster,
Grand Master of Ireland 1770,
1771 and 1771. The Royal Arch
jewel he is wearing is now in the
Grand Lodge collection,
London.

103 **Right**
An Irish Past Master's jewel in silver and paste by James Brush and Sons.

104 **Below**
The Grand Lodge Room in Freemasons' Hall, Dublin, built 1869.

Belfast lodges returned their allegiance to the Grand Lodge in Dublin. In 1811 the Grand Lodge began to assert its authority and threatened to suspend or revoke the Warrants of rebellious lodges. Not surprisingly, many reaffirmed their allegiance to the Dublin Grand Lodge. By 1813 the rebellion had failed, and Seton was exposed as the fraud he was both in Masonic circles and in the civil courts. The Grand East of Ulster held its last meeting in 1814.

Irish Freemasonry faced the threat of extinction in 1823. As a result of the aftermath of the French Revolution various Bills had been enacted banning the meetings of seditious or secret societies. Freemasonry as a moral and philanthropic organization, demonstrably loyal to the rule of law and the crown, had been specifically exempted from the provisions of the various acts, especially the Unlawful Societies Act of 1799. In 1823 an Unlawful Oaths in Ireland Act was passed in which no specific exemption of Freemasonry was mentioned. Conscious of their civil and Masonic duties to uphold the law, the Grand Lodge of Ireland ordered all of its lodges to cease working until the situation was resolved. The 3rd Duke of Leinster (Grand Master 1813-74) immediately sought clarification, pointing out Freemasonry's exemption under the 1799 Act. The Government responded ten months later by announcing that they had not intended Freemasonry to be covered by the 1823 Act and that they were

105
Bicentenary of the Grand Lodge of Ireland, 1926. The Earl of Donoughmore, Grand Master, with delegations from England, Scotland and other Grand Lodges.

still exempt from such legislation under the terms of the 1799 Act. This was, of course, happy news for Irish Freemasonry but it came too late for a number of the country lodges which, having obeyed the Grand Lodge order to cease meeting, never opened their doors again. The events of 1823 were also to lead to a resurgence of anti-Masonic feeling amongst the Roman Catholic hierarchy in Ireland, which also prevented a number of lodges reopening.

It appears to surprise many that Freemasonry flourished in Ireland, a predominantly Catholic country, particularly after the issue of the various Papal Bulls condemning Freemasonry. This was largely due to the religious situation in Ireland—an established Anglican State Church with Roman Catholics barely tolerated and, under the terms of the Test Act of 1693, unable to hold even minor official posts. The Papal Bulls of 1737 and 1751 were largely ignored in Ireland until they were enacted by Archbishop Troy of Dublin in the wake of the French Revolution and the lunatic ravings of Robison and the Abbé Baruel. Even this official recognition by the Irish Catholic Church of the papal condemnation of Freemasonry did not prevent Irish Catholics, including the great patriot and champion of Catholic Emancipation, Daniel O'Connell, from becoming Freemasons. The activity over the 1823 Act added fuel to the Irish Catholic Church's fire and priests began to enforce sanctions against Catholics who continued in Freemasonry, leading to a decline in Catholic

106 **Above left**
Burns was a member of the Craft, Royal Arch and Knights Templar and wrote some Masonic verse. Scott was initiated in 1801.

107 **Left**
The inauguration of Robert Burns as the Poet Laureate of the Lodge Canongate Kilwinning, Edinburgh.

108 **Above**
Grand Lodge of Scotland laying the Foundation Stone of the New College, Edinburgh, 1789.

membership which had been in the majority in the early 1800s.

The return of Mother Kilwinning and her lodges to the Grand Lodge of Scotland in 1807 healed a breach of seventy years but caused further problems. Mother Kilwinning claimed to be the oldest Scottish lodge and demanded to head the Scottish list of lodges. The Lodge of Edinburgh (Mary's Chapel) No. 1 could prove its existence as far back as at least 1599. Its members objected to their 'seniority' being usurped by Mother Kilwinning and an unseemly wrangle ensued. The Lodge of Edinburgh stated that it would only agree if Mother Kilwinning could prove it was the older lodge. During the ensuing argument a number of lodges seceded from the Grand Lodge of Scotland and formed a body styling itself 'The Associated Lodges seceding from the present Grand Lodge of Scotland'.

Whilst the Mother Kilwinning argument was in progress more discussion occurred as a result of actions by Dr John Mitchell, Master of

109 **Opposite**
Large painted apron of a member of the Lodge Scoon and Perth No. 3 c.1830.

110
A nineteenth-century Scottish Lodge Master in his regalia.

111 Above
Honorary membership certificate of the Lodge of Edinburgh (Mary's Chapel) No. 2 presented to HRH Albert Edward, Prince of Wales, 12 October 1870.

112 Right
Symbolic charts, either hand-painted (as here) or engraved were very popular in Britain in the 1830s and 1840s. They were used either as aides-mémoires *or purely for decoration.*

113 Far right
Edward VII, as Prince of Wales, in his regalia as Grand Master of the United Grand Lodge of England, 1874-1901.

Lodge Caledonian. In 1807 he proposed in the Grand Lodge that an address be presented to King George III, not a Freemason himself, thanking him for supporting the established Church (the King had publicly opposed Catholic Emancipation). Happily, the motion was defeated for it was highly un-Masonic, breaking the landmark rule that Freemasonry as a body does not involve itself in or comment upon religion. Dr Mitchell was furious, repeatedly proposed to his Lodge Caledonian that they should withdraw from the Grand Lodge, and as a result was hauled up before the Grand Lodge in 1808 and expelled from the Craft. At the same time a number of his associates in Lodge Caledonian, Lodge of Edinburgh, and the Lodge of St Andrew were suspended. A feud developed and civil litigation ensued. Unwisely, the Prince of Wales, then Grand Master Mason, was persuaded to intervene and the resulting injudicious correspondence was made public in the courts and ordered to be burnt by the public hangman. It was not until 1813 that all the disputes were healed. The Grand Lodge was forced to give way on most matters, Mother Kilwinning was placed at the head of the list with the number '0', the only loser seemed to be Dr Mitchell whose sentence of expulsion was not withdrawn.

After the turmoil Freemasonry in the British Isles settled down in the 1830s and began a period of consolidation and quiet expansion. The industrial revolution and the improvement of transport with the coming of the railways had their effects. In the new industrial towns many new lodges were founded. Before the coming of the railways lodge membership had been very localized but rail transport meant that people could travel more easily to other lodges, better links could be made between lodges within a particular province, and better communications between provincial lodges and Grand Lodge could be forged.

An even greater spur to expansion was the emergence of a new Prince of Wales as a Masonic leader. On the death of the Duke of Sussex in 1843 Freemasonry went through a period when it had no royal participation. The only adult royal male was the Prince Consort (Fig. 111), who appears to have shown no interest in Freemasonry. Queen Victoria is reputed to have been unfavourable to Freemasonry, which may have led to her husband standing apart from it. It was this alleged view held by the Queen that is supposed to have led to Albert Edward, Prince of Wales not to seek initiation in England but to have come into Freemasonry in Sweden, where he was initiated by the King of Sweden in December 1869. Queen Victoria's reaction is not recorded but her son must have persuaded her that Freemasonry was beneficial for she ultimately became patron of and a regular donor to the Masonic charities. The Craft's reaction to the Prince of Wales's initiation was one of great pleasure. He was immediately elected a Past Grand Master in England and was installed as Protector of

114 **Opposite**
The Prince of Wales, as Grand Master, laying the Foundation Stone of Truro Cathedral with Masonic ceremonies, 1880.

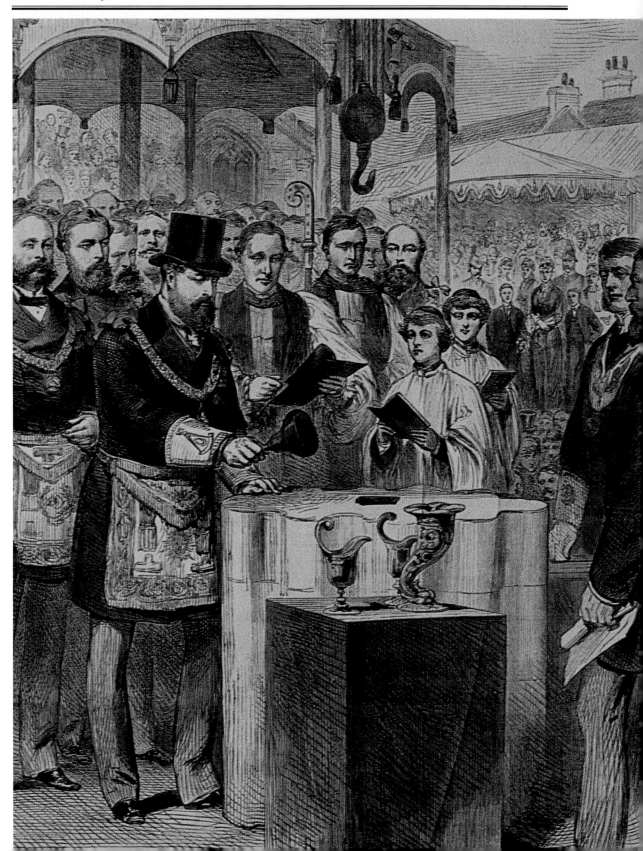

115 Above
The close ties which have always existed between the Grand Lodges of England, Ireland and Scotland are illustrated in this souvenir lithograph of the three Grand Masters.

116 Right
The lodge room at Lahore, c.1900, in which Rudyard Kipling attended meetings.

117 Far right
Dorabjee P. Cama. A Parsee who became the first Indian Grand Officer when he was appointed Grand Treasurer in 1886.

118
Indian silver box by Jellicoe,
Calcutta, 1875. Presented to
Albert Edward, Prince of
Wales, by the Masons of
Calcutta.

119 **Opposite**
Freemasons' Hall, Collins
Street, Melbourne, home of the
United Grand Lodge of
Victoria. An artist's impression.

Freemasonry in both the Irish and the Scottish Grand Lodges.

A crisis occurred in the United Grand Lodge of England in September 1874. The Grand Master, the Marquess of Ripon, had converted to Roman Catholicism and in view of the papacy's recent reiteration of its abhorrence of Freemasonry, Ripon felt that he could not, in conscience, continue as Grand Master, although he personally found no incompatibility between his religion and Freemasonry. Consternation reigned but the Deputy Grand Master, the Earl of Carnarvon, came up with the ideal solution. He offered to approach the Prince of Wales to enquire if he would be willing for his name to go forward for election as Grand Master. The Prince agreed with alacrity and was elected by acclamation in December 1874 (Figs. 113-4). The Prince was to be a great publicist of Freemasonry. As well as being actively involved as Grand Master and a member of various lodges, wherever he travelled within the British Isles or abroad he attended meetings or had social events arranged at which he would meet the local Freemasons. The twenty-six years of his Grand Mastership were to see a great expansion of Freemasonry, particularly in the colonies.

The early nineteenth century saw a steady expansion of Freemasonry in the old imperial territories—Canada, the West Indies, and India. The great explorations of the century, which opened up Africa, the Far East, and Australasia, led to the introduction of Freemasonry into these areas as they were gradually settled. All three of the British Grand Lodges worked harmoniously together setting up first lodges, then districts in the new territories. As in the eighteenth century, they were followed by the

Dutch and the French, particularly in the West Indies, Africa, and the Far East.

In India, Freemasonry went from strength to strength. As the numbers of military personnel and civil servants grew so did the number of English, Irish, and Scottish lodges. In some cases the lodges were short lived, depending upon military conditions. Increasingly from the 1830s, natives were admitted to the lodges. As mentioned earlier, at first there was a problem over the admission of Hindus, because of the mistaken belief that Hinduism is a polytheistic religion. An appeal was made to the Duke of Sussex who insisted that the lodges admit Hindus, knowing well that the various 'gods' of the Hindus were not separate gods but personifications of characteristics of one central deity. Freemasonry had a great appeal to the Indians, who joined in great numbers. As Kipling and others were later to point out in their writings, whatever quarrels there may have been between the various Indian religious groups and between Indians and the British, they all met on an equal footing in lodge.

It was the Irish who introduced Freemasonry into Australia. The earliest recorded Masonic meeting took place in Sydney in 1803 when 'several officers of His Majesty's ships together with some respectable inhabitants of Sydney' met together. The meeting was apparently held against the orders of the Governor and several of those present were arrested. From 1816 onwards there were several Irish travelling military lodges meeting in New South Wales, but it was not until 1820 that the first stationary lodge was warranted—the Australian Social Lodge No. 260 of the Irish Constitution (now the Lodge of Antiquity No. 1 of the United Grand Lodge of New South Wales). The first lodge for South Australia was warranted in 1834 as the South Australian Lodge of Friendship. Formed by Freemasons planning to emigrate to South Australia, it was constituted and held its first meetings in London before being taken to Adelaide. Tasmania began its masonic history with an Irish Lodge in 1828; Victoria with an English lodge in 1841 (Fig. 119); Western Australia with an English lodge in 1842; and Queensland with an English lodge in 1859, the year it was separated from New South Wales as a new State. English Freemasons introduced Freemasonry into New Zealand in 1842. The Irish followed in 1843 and for a number of years there was a group of French lodges.

In the Far East, a lodge was established in Penang in 1809 but it met infrequently. British Freemasonry became firmly established with the formation of Zetland-in-the-East Lodge in Singapore in 1845. British lodges were established throughout Malaysia. In 1844 the Royal Sussex Lodge was formed in Canton, beginning the development of British Freemasonry in the Chinese ports and Hong Kong (Fig. 120). From here the English and Scottish introduced Freemasonry into Japan.

Freemasonry had been introduced into the Philippines by the Portuguese but did not take root until after the Spanish-American War of 1898, when regular lodges were warranted by the Scottish and some American Grand Lodges and irregular Freemasonry was introduced by the French and Spanish. As in India, Freemasonry in the Far East quickly became multiracial and had members representing all the religions practised in the area.

Although the English Grand Lodge had had Provincial Grand Masters for ports on the West Coast of Africa in the eighteenth century it was the Dutch who first established successful lodges, at Capetown in 1772 and 1803, leading to a flourishing Dutch Provincial Grand Lodge for Southern Africa which, in 1960, was to become the independent Grand Lodge of South Africa. The British followed with the establishment of an English lodge in 1813. The development of Freemasonry in southern Africa parallels the progressive opening up and settlement of the area. In the north of the continent the British, French, and Italians all had lodges in Egypt, some of which seceded to form various Grand Lodges and Grand Orients, all of which were short-lived (Fig. 121). East and West Africa were largely colonized in the late nineteenth and early twentieth centuries, and as in other colonies Freemasonry arrived with the settlers and administrators.

120
Freemasons' Hall, Shanghai, opened in 1931 and serving the English, Irish and Scottish Masons in the International Settlement.

1924

121 **Far left**
Prince Mohamed Aly was the
last Grand Master of Egypt.
The National Grand Lodge
became embroiled in politics,
had its recognition withdrawn,
and disintegrated in the 1930s.

122
John, 1st Earl of Durham in his
regalia as Pro Grand Master,
1839. As John George Lambton
his report on Canada led to the
political settlement of Canada
and the achievement of
Dominion status.

123
An open-air meeting of Cariboo Lodge No. 4, Vancouver in 1869.

As was said in Chapter 3, the development of British Freemasonry outside the British Isles closely followed the development of the Empire. But empires are like families, with its colonies as children, and children grow to adulthood and look for independence. Just as the colonies sought political independence from Britain so, in many areas, the lodges sought Masonic independence from the home Grand Lodges. The first to go were the American lodges, and their going was so painless as to have been almost unnoticed. Indeed the English Lodges remained on the register until the two registers were combined after the union of 1813. The colonies having won their independence, the lodges within each of the new states of the United States simply joined together to form state-based Grand Lodges.

In other countries the process was not so simple. After the United States the next territory to feel the stirrings of Masonic independence was Canada. By the 1850s the English lodges in Lower Canada (Ontario) were complaining of neglect by the Grand Lodge administration and the need to remit fees and dues to London. There was a certain justness in their claims. The Grand Secretary, William White, had been in office for nearly

fifty years, was over eighty years old and largely neglected correspondence from overseas. Finding no answers to their grievances the Ontario authorities by-passed the Grand Secretary and appealed to the Grand Master and other senior members. A Committee of Enquiry was immediately set up. Its workings were slow, however, and the Canadians forced the issue by deciding to proclaim their independence and setting up a Grand Lodge of Canada in 1856. Faced with a *fait accompli*, the English Grand Lodge, after much discussion, recognized the new Grand Lodge, set up a Colonial Board to deal with all matters offering lodges abroad, and quietly retired the Grand Secretary.

Realizing that other colonial lodges would inevitably follow the Ontario lodges, the English, Irish, and Scottish Grand Lodges consulted together to devise a system for avoiding the acrimony that had surrounded the Canadian question. It was jointly decided that, if a call for independence came, plebiscites should be held in all the lodges. If the majority within a lodge opted for independence, then the vote of that lodge was for independence. If a majority of lodges were for independence, then the new Grand Lodge would be accepted *provided* that any lodge that wished

124
Officers and members of the Star of Agra Lodge No. 1936, Bengal, c.1927.

to remain under the jurisdiction of the home Grand Lodge that had warranted it was allowed to continue to work without interference from the new Grand Lodge. In return for this guarantee the home Grand Lodges would regard the territory of the new Grand Lodge as closed and would not issue warrants for any new lodges within that territory. By this means further Grand Lodges emerged in Canada, and the States Grand Lodges in Australia and the Grand Lodge of New Zealand came into being. The system was fair and has worked, all the Commonwealth Grand Lodges being in perfect amity with the home Grand Lodges. Not all the lodges opted for independence. In New Zealand four constitutions work happily together: the Grand Lodge of New Zealand, two English Districts, and a number of Irish and Scottish lodges. The same situation applies in India, where a Grand Lodge was formed in 1961. In Canada the English lodges of Newfoundland have rejected the idea of a local Grand Lodge on a number of occasions, preferring to remain a District Grand Lodge under the United Grand Lodge of England.

125
Arthur, Duke of Connaught,
Grand Master 1901-39,
processing through Bulawayo,
Zimbabwe, to lay the
Foundation Stone of the
Presbyterian Church.

The three home Grand Lodges still have a large number of lodges abroad. The United Grand Lodge of England has the following District Grand Lodges (the number in brackets following each name is the number of lodges within the district): Cyprus (7); Gibraltar (9); Bengal (24); Bombay (23); Burma (9); Eastern Archipelago (28); Hong Kong and the Far East (33); Madras (18); Northern India (5); Sri Lanka (9); East Africa (37); Ghana (47); Natal (46); Nigeria (4 districts with 27); Orange Free State (11); Sierra Leone and the Gambia (14); South Africa (3 districts with 92); South West Africa (6); Transvaal (121); Zambia (15); Zimbabwe (31); Bahamas and Turks (8); Barbados and the Eastern Caribbean (13); Jamaica (21); Newfoundland (27); South America, Northern Division (11); South America Southern Division (13); Trinidad (7); North Island New Zealand (23); South Island New Zealand (17). In addition, there are Inspectorates of Bermuda (5); Malta (2); Montreal and Halifax (3), and South West Pacific (6); and individual lodges in Australia (4); Bangladesh; Zante; Monte Carlo; Curacao; New Guinea; St Helena, and Dominica. The District Grand Lodge of Pakistan (14) has been in abeyance since 1967 when the government banned Freemasonry.

The Grand Lodge of Ireland has overseas provinces in: New Zealand (4 lodges); South Africa Northern (31); Southern Cape Province (11); Natal (15); Zimbabwe (8); India (10); Nigeria (14); Ghana (18); Zambia (6). There are also lodges in Pakistan (1); Sri Lanka (3); Malta (2); Gibraltar (1); Bermuda (4); Jamaica (2); Hong Kong (3); Kuala Lumpar (1); Singapore (1); Kenya (1); Sierra Leone (1); and South Australia (1).

Scotland has District Grand Lodges in: Barbados (6 lodges); Eastern India (3); Eastern Province, Cape of Good Hope (14); Far East (10); Ghana (29); Gibraltar (3); Guyana (5); Jamaica and The Bahamas (20); Middle East (10); Natal (25); Newfoundland (16); New Zealand North (4); New Zealand South (7); Nigeria (65); Sierra Leone and the Gambia (14); Transvaal, Orange Free State and Northern Cape (104); Trinidad and Tobago (11); Western Australia (8); Western Australia Goldfields (7); Western India (26); Western Province of the Cape of Good Hope (15); Zambia (12); and Zimbabwe (22). There are groups under Grand Superintendents in Bermuda (3); Chile and Peru (6); and East Africa (6). In addition there are Scottish lodges in Belgium (2); Botswana (2); Fiji (1); Jordan (2); Malawi (4); Malta (1); Mauritius (1); Philippines (1); Panama (2); Sri Lanka (1); Togo (1) and St Kitts (1).

Charity is one of the three great principles of Freemasonry and the British Grand Lodges have practised it from their earliest days. Individual lodges usually have their own benevolent funds to give immediate relief to their members or dependants, but there are also major centralized charities looking after special groups. The first was established in England in 1789 when the Chevalier Bartholomew Ruspini, Surgeon Dentist to

King George III, and others collected money to build a school to educate the daughters of indigent or deceased Freemasons (Fig. 127). A similar charity for boys was formed in 1798 but rather than building a school it gave grants to clothe and educate boys, a school eventually being built in 1856. The two charities later became the Royal Masonic Institution for Girls and the Royal Masonic Institution for Boys. In the 1830s a project was begun to build an 'asylum for aged and decayed Freemasons'. The project did not have the approval of the Grand Master, who instituted an annuity scheme. Happily, the two were united in 1842 to form the Royal Masonic Benevolent Institution, which provided annuities or residential care for elderly Freemasons, widows and dependants. During the First World War an old hospital in the Fulham Road in London was taken over as the Freemasons' War Hospital and Nursing Home (Fig. 128). So successful was the scheme that funds were raised to build a permanent hospital. In 1933 the Royal Masonic Hospital at Ravenscourt Park, London, was opened by King George V and Queen Mary.

The Grand Lodge of Ireland drew up rules for a Central Committee of Charity in 1739. As in England, it was funded by contributions from

126 **Left**
Pandit Motilal Nehru, father of the Indian Prime Minister, in regalia as a District Grand Deacon of Bengal.

127 **Above**
A girls' school was opened in 1789. The girls are here paraded before the Prince of Wales and other Freemasons in Sandby's Grand Hall in Freemasons Hall, London.

lodges and many theatrical benefit performances. In 1792 a fund for orphan girls was started which was taken over and managed by the Grand Lodge in 1799. The Masonic Female Orphan School was opened in 1802. It was not until 1869 that a similar scheme was started for boys, the first Boys School being purchased in 1878. Both schools were closed down in the 1970s. Proceeds from the sales were formed into a trust which provides educational welfare grants for girls and boys. In 1887 the Victoria Jubilee Masonic Annuity Fund was started to provide annuities for elderly brethren and widows.

In Scotland, until the Fund of Masonic Benevolence was formed in 1846, most lodges had benefit societies attached to them. Collections were regularly taken at Grand Lodge meetings which went into the Grand Lodge Charity Fund. An Annuity Fund was established in 1888 to look after the elderly and widows. In 1917 an Orphan Annuity Fund was started. In 1957 a house, Ault Wharrie, in Dunblane, was purchased as an old people's home. A further house, Randolph Hill, was purchased and in 1967 new building was commenced to provide accommodation for married couples. To these have been added Sir James McKay House, Edinburgh, and the Marcus Humphrey Home, Bridge of Weir.

The great Masonic charities developed in a period when there was no welfare state. With the coming of that system many of the needs the Masonic charities had filled were taken over by the state. As a result, in the 1970s the present Grand Master of England, HRH the Duke of Kent, set up a committee to see how the monies raised by the charities could best be expended. As a result, the Girls and Boys Institutions were combined as the Masonic Trust for Girls and Boys, which provides educational and welfare grants to over a thousand children. An attempt to combine the Benevolent Institution and Hospital into a Trust for the Aged and Sick was not successful. The Royal Masonic Benevolent Institution now runs seventeen homes for the elderly in England and Wales. The Grand Lodge Board of Benevolence became the independent Grand Charity in 1980 and has three functions: to relieve Masonic petitioners and their dependants; to act as a central channel for funds to Masonic charities; and to make major and minor grants to non-Masonic charities.

In the matter of Charity, Freemasonry has often been accused of simply raising money for its own members, like a benefit society or insurance club. Nothing could be further from the truth. As early as 1731 English lodges raised money to enable poor families to join General Oglethorpe in settling the American Colony of Georgia. In 1737 the Grand Lodge of Scotland paid the wages of operative masons building the Edinburgh Infirmary. At the same time they paid for the apprenticeships of a number of orphans of operative masons. During the Napoleonic Wars all three British Grand Lodges provided funds to assist British prisoners of war in

128
*The original Freemasons'
Hospital and Nursing Home in
Fulham Road, London, c.1918.*

Europe and French prisoners of war in the British Isles. In modern times the United Grand Lodge of England raised over £600,000 in celebration of its 250th anniversary in 1967. A trust was set up, the income of which is administered by the Royal College of Surgeons and has funded a great deal of research into cancer and heart disease. Each year since 1980 the Grand Charity has funded a major project, from medical research to providing the thirteenth Masonic lifeboat for the Royal National Lifeboat Institution (Fig. 129), founding a Chair of Gerontology in the University of Cambridge, and funding research and welfare projects in the area of drug abuse. Large sums have been sent to national and international disaster relief funds. Each year up to £100,000 is given in donations of £500 or £1000 to a long list of national medical and welfare charities. What is not often known is that all of this money is raised within Freemasonry itself without public appeals or street collections. Furthermore, Charity is not simply giving money; it also involves the giving of time and talents. In many areas lodges will adopt a children's home, old people's home or hospital, and members regularly visit the residents, take them out, or provide comforts.

Until the post-war era British Freemasonry was relatively free from anti-Masonry. In the early days of organized Freemasonry there was a healthy public curiosity about Masonic ceremonies which was satisfied by the publication of what purported to be exposures of Masonic ritual. Throughout the eighteenth century cartoons appeared lampooning 'the secrets' of Masonry. In London in the 1730s and 1740s a group of mock

129
The RNLI Lifeboat Duchess of Kent presented by the Grand Charity in 1980. The thirteenth lifeboat presented to the RNLI by English Freemasonry.

Masons, the Scald Miserable Masons, organized public processions mocking the Grand Master's procession to the Annual Feast. A few parsons preached against the 'Godless sect' of Freemasonry, in the erroneous belief that Freemasonry was some form of Deistic religion set up as a rival to the established Anglican Church. In 1756 the Synod of the We Free Presbyterians in Scotland, a very minor Presbyterian sect, banned its members from Freemasonry on pain of excommunication. Freemasons who wished to remain members of this Church had to prostrate themselves publicly before the communion table, abjure their Masonic obligations, and do public penance for their 'sin'. The action of the 'We Free's' had little effect in Scotland and went unnoticed elsewhere. That Freemasonry was not regarded as a secret or a subversive society by the government or by parliament is clearly shown by its specific exclusion from the terms of the 1799 Unlawful Societies Act, which declared illegal any organization requiring its members to take an oath or obligation. Throughout the nineteenth and early twentieth centuries British Freemasonry was largely untroubled by anti-Masonry.

In the immediate post-war period the Revd Walton Hannah, an Anglican cleric who appears to have regarded Freemasonry as the anti-

131
Cartoonists in the 18th century found the 'secrets' of Freemasonry a popular subject for a lampoon. The above is a typical example.

130 **Opposite**
Engraving of Hogarth's Night. Hogarth, himself a Freemason, satirizes the inebriated Master being helped home by the Tyler.

Christ, appeared on the scene. As a result of various articles by Hannah the subject of Freemasonry was raised in the General Assembly of the Church of England in 1951. A motion to have a full investigation of Freemasonry was heavily defeated (only one person voted in its favour). Hannah then went on to produce a book, *Darkness Visible*, claiming that Freemasonry was an anti-Christian religion practising heresies and blasphemy. The appearance of the book caused a two-week sensation in the press. In addition to religious comment, disgruntled non-Masons for the first time began to accuse Freemasonry of being some form of conspiracy. In 1965 James Dewar produced a programme for BBC Television which took up the conspiracy theory and enacted, inaccurately, some of the more dramatic parts of the ritual. Again there was a flurry of accusations in the media, which rapidly died down. Such was not the case in 1984 when the late Stephen Knight's *The Brotherhood* appeared.

Knight claimed that his book was an impartial and seriously researched study, in spite of the fact that at no time did he approach, even indirectly, any of the Masonic authorities in the British Isles. Using hearsay, legend, pseudonymous and anonymous 'evidence', Knight claimed that Freemasonry was an anti-Christian religion of occult origins; that a secret cabal within, and largely unknown to, Freemasonry at least influenced it, if it did not actually control all aspects of British life; that jobs and promotion within the legal profession, the police, and most other professions depended upon membership of Freemasonry; that a Freemason's obligations meant that he had to support a fellow Freemason regardless of the circumstances or legal position; that Freemasons were at the heart of most of the corruption in public life in the post-war years; and that English Freemasonry had been or was ripe for infiltration by the KGB as a future means of destabilizing British life. Whatever one thinks of the content, Knight's book was an 'easy read', like a detective novel or a spy story. It was immediately taken up by the media and for over two years Freemasonry was hardly ever out of the news. *The Brotherhood* acted as a catalyst for many disgruntled individuals and groups who saw Freemasonry as a whipping boy for their own or the world's ills. Many groups joined in the fray. The Methodist and Anglican Churches in England; the Church of Scotland; the Metropolitan Police; a number of local authorities, and various national and local politicians.

The anti-Masonic activity in England in the period 1984-7 begs the questions why did it come about and why did the public believe the nonsense that appeared in books and the media? There is no doubt that one of the major reasons had been the attitude of the United Grand Lodge of England itself. Until the late 1930s Freemasonry had been, and more importantly *was seen* to be, an ordinary part of English social life. Meetings at all levels were reported in the national and local press; two weekly

RAN-POP "
ERIES

132
Postcard manufacturers in the early 20th century produced a number of sets poking gentle fun at Freemasonry. The above is from the Granpop series, probably the most popular.

Masonic newspapers and a monthly magazine were on public sale; Masons in their regalia took part in public processions; many foundation stones of public structures were laid with Masonic ceremonial and public participation; Freemasons were known in the local communities. For reasons unknown, English Freemasonry then began to turn in on itself and develop an attitude of intense privacy. The coming of the Second World War intensified this attitude, there being a general fostering of privacy as a result of a fear of spies and fifth columnists. When the war was over and society in general returned to normality, Freemasonry remained secretive. As a result, English Freemasonry separated itself from the society in which it existed. Non-Masons who had no contact with Freemasonry through family or friends were in many cases not aware of its existence until the media brought it to their attention. Combined with, and part of, the privacy issue was the United Grand Lodge of England's practice of not commenting on any outside statements on Freemasonry. Initially this policy worked. Without comment there can be no dialogue and, as happened with the General Assembly debate of 1951 and the BBC Television programme of 1965, the lack of comment led to the subject being dropped by the media within a few days. Times change, however, and today 'no comment' is taken as an admission that there is something in what has been said or written—the 'no smoke without fire' attitude.

In 1984 the United Grand Lodge of England altered its traditional policy of 'no comment' to one of limited comment, the correction of factual errors, and the dissemination of correct information to counter the nonsense written by certain types of journalists. In particular, the following topics have been dealt with:

Secrecy: Freemasonry is not a secret society. Its *Aims and Relationships* have been published. Its rule book (the *Book of Constitutions*) is on public sale. Its headquarters in London is open to the public. There is no requirement for a Freemason to conceal his membership.

Religion: Freemasonry is not a religion, a substitute for religion, or an attempt to combine religions in one super religion. Whilst it is essential for every candidate for Freemasonry to have a belief in a Supreme Being, how he expresses that belief is up to him. Freemasonry deals in relations between men not the relationship between man and God, which is the preserve of religion. Religion may not be discussed at Masonic meetings.

Politics: Freemasonry is apolitical. Like religion, a Freemason's political opinions are his own and no business of his lodge. Freemasons as individuals have their own political views but neither an individual lodge nor a Grand Lodge can have a political view or involve itself in politics.

Law: A Freemason is obligated to uphold the laws of the land in which he resides. Breaking the laws is a Masonic offence and subject to Masonic discipline, which according to the severity of the offence can lead from temporary suspension of membership to permanent exclusion from Freemasonry as a whole.

Duty: A Freemason's prime duties are to his God, the law, his family, and society in general. His duties towards Freemasonry in general and individual Freemasons come very much after his prime duties. A Freemason's obligations to a fellow Freemason are very clearly defined and must be 'without detriment to himself or his connections'. Anyone who claims that Freemasons obligate themselves to assist fellow Freemasons regardless of the circumstances or the legal position is lying. The third degree obligation states quite specifically that in the case of 'murder, treason, felony, and all other offences contrary to the laws of God or the ordnances of the realm' a Freemason may *not* assist or protect a fellow member.

6

The Nineteenth Century in Europe

I N ENGLAND the fusion of the two rival Grand Lodges pre-ceded the end of the Napoleonic Wars by two years and ushered in, for Freemasonry in the British Isles, a period of peaceful progress, marred only by occasional small and, usually, local Masonic disputes. Matters were very different in continental Europe, where political stability came slowly. France and Italy, especially, were riven by political turmoil and, in the latter case, by a long and bitter struggle for unification and complete freedom from both foreign and papal domination. French and Italian Masons identified themselves with the struggle for freedom and in both countries the Craft played an active role on the 'progressive' side of the political divide.

In Italy, Freemasonry had led a chequered existence—alternately permitted or suppressed according to the feelings of the current political masters of the city or region concerned. But as the country was gradually united under Victor Emmanuel of Sardinia, becoming, in 1859, the Kingdom of Italy, so Freemasonry was universally re-established. Masonic activities, however were directed by four quite distinct bodies—the Grand Orient and Grand Lodge of Italy, the two Supreme Councils—which were not united until 1873 when the Grand Orient of Italy was accepted by all as the sole governing body of Italian Freemasonry. And while these moved towards union, so the Church became ever more implacably hostile— which, given that the leaders of Italian Freemasonry were Mazzini and Garibaldi, who had been instrumental in wresting the Papal States and Rome itself from the Church's temporal rule, was scarcely surprising. It led, however, to the perpetuation of an unfortunate anti-clerical attitude within Italian Freemasonry as a whole, which may be summed up in the

133-4 **Opposite**
Two figures showing French Masonic dress c.*1820 from a set of watercolours entitled* Atlas du Rite Ecossais Ancien et Accepté.

135 **Above**
*Duc Elie de Cases. Sovereign
Grand Commander of the
Supreme Council of France
1818-21 and 1838-60.*

136
*There is no documentary
evidence that Napoleon was a
Freemason, but he placed his
family in senior offices in French
Freemasonry on its revival after
the Revolution.*

words of a later Grand Master, Ernesto Nathan: 'Never have we attacked a religion, but we are the sworn enemies of the clerical parties, that is to say, those parties that make use of religion in order to throw Italy into bondage once more.'

Anti-clericalism was also destined to become a prominent and permanent feature of Freemasonry in France, if for rather more philosophical than practical reasons. During the turbulent years following the

Revolution of 1789, French Freemasonry had all but ceased to exist. The Grand Orient did not commence its revival until 1795, closely followed by the much smaller Grand Lodge, but by 1799 it had united with its rival, although it was not until many years after this that most of the other Masonic bodies active in France (mostly of *Ecossais* origin) also joined the Grand Orient. Some of them never did. In 1804 the Comte de Grasse-Tilly established a Supreme Council of the Ancient and Accepted Scottish

137
Marc Bedaride in the collar of Grand Master of the Order of Misraim.

Rite in France that initially worked in harmony with the Grand Orient, but after the Supreme Council's revival in 1821 (it had been dormant since the fall of Napoleon in 1814) there ensued a long period of bitter rivalry and mutual recrimination until 1841 when a pact was concluded by which each recognized the jurisdiction of the other. Both bodies, however, had been plagued by two irregular but highly successful Masonic rites that were destined to be a cause of constant irritation in France and elsewhere for many years: the Rites of Misraim and of Memphis.

The Rite of Misraim was the brainchild of one Lechangeur who

138
A typical French Craft apron of the early 19th century. Watercolour sketch from a manufacturer's pattern book.

concocted a system of ninety degrees in Italy in 1805. He was joined by a number of French Masons, among whom were the three brothers Bedarride who in 1813 transported the Rite to France, where it spread rapidly with the support of certain prominent members of the Ancient and Accepted Scottish Rite. But the Bedarride brothers treated the Rite as a source of income and there was considerable friction between them and their disciples, as well as strife with the Grand Orient. As a consequence of this, the Rite of Misraim became dormant in 1822, was revived in 1830, and staggered on until 1856 when Michel Bedarride (Fig. 137) was

139
Joseph Bonaparte in the collar of a Grand Officer of the Grand Orient of France.

Lith. de Delpech à Paris.

succeeded by Dr Hayere—a more honourable Grand Master who brought new life to the Rite and built it up into a successful, if somewhat strange and esoteric, Masonic body.

Its companion rite, that of Memphis, was in many ways more disreputable. It appeared at Paris in 1838 as a system of ninety-seven degrees, full of esoteric symbolism, and under the control of J.E. Marconis de Negre who had, for reasons that are not clear, been earlier expelled from the Rite of Misraim. Marconis (who styled himself Grand Hierophant) claimed that the Rite had been founded at Cairo in 1814 by one Samuel Honis who brought it to France in the following year and, with the help of Marconis's father, founded a Lodge at Montauban. The Rite then promptly fell into abeyance for twenty-three years, but its revival was short-lived: in 1840 Memphis lodges were closed by the police, to be reopened in 1849 and closed again in 1852. Marconis then moved the Rite to London and exported it to the United States of America, whence it returned to France to be absorbed by the Grand Orient in 1862 and gently smothered. In Britain it survived—to the irritation of United Grand Lodge—as the Antient and Primitive Rite, taking Misraim under its wing in 1875.

Although an insignificant body in itself, the Rite of Memphis illustrates in its history the ease with which more or less irregular bodies could be established in France—especially when they claimed to propagate esoteric wisdom. But the esoteric strand was only one of a number that made up French Freemasonry; another, and far more significant, was the anti-clerical stand.

After 1841 the Grand Orient and the Supreme Council maintained a degree of amity and after the establishment of the Republic in 1848 they worked together to suppress a fledgling Grand Lodge that sought to model itself on the United Grand Lodge of England. The Grand Orient then reconstituted itself and in its new Constitutions of 1849 laid down unequivocally that 'the basis of Freemasonry is a belief in God and in the immortality of the soul, and the solidarity of humanity'. It did not, however, espouse internal democracy: in 1852 Prince Lucien Murat was elected Grand Master and for ten years he subjected the Grand Orient to arbitrary government. A more democratic regime ensued after 1862 when the Emperor Napoleon III appointed Marshal Magnan in Murat's place, but following the revolution of 1871 the office of Grand Master was abolished, being replaced by a President of the Council. There followed, too, an upsurge of anti-clericalism, the effect of which was to lead in 1877 to the dramatic change in the Constitution whereby all reference to God was removed and the first article rephrased to read 'Its Freemasonry's basis is in absolute liberty of Conscience and the solidarity of Humanity'. God was also, necessarily, expunged from the three Craft rituals. The reason

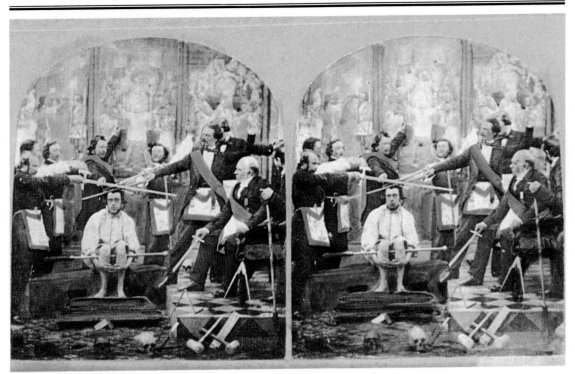

for this drastic action was to ensure that the Craft 'excludes no person on account of his beliefs', but it violated the first and most important ancient landmark of the order, which demands a belief in the Grand Architect of the Universe—that is, in God.

The United Grand Lodge of England, in common with the Scottish, Irish, and most North American Grand Lodges, immediately severed all connection with the Grand Orient and pointed out that it could not recognize as 'true and genuine' brethren any who had been initiated 'in lodges which either deny or ignore that belief. This prohibition extended also to the Grand Independent Symbolic Lodge, which broke away from the French Supreme Council in 1880 in order to work the three Craft degrees, because its constitutions neatly avoided any reference to God. With all governing bodies of the Craft thus making themselves irregular, 1877 became the year in which regular Freemasonry in France ceased to exist. It would not reappear until 1913.

There can be no doubt that the virtual declaration of irreligion by the Grand Orient, coupled with its endemic anti-clericalism and the virulent hostility to the Church shown by Italian Masons, led directly to Pope Leo XIII issuing in 1884 his Encyclical *Humanum Genus*, the most damning and vitriolic of all papal attacks on Freemasonry. Freemasons, said Leo, 'follow the evil one' and Masonry has as its aim 'the desire of overthrowing

140
Stereoscope photograph, hand-coloured. One of a series of French provenance, exposing the 'secrets' of Freemasonry.

TO ALL GODLy PEOPLE,
in the Citie of
LONDON.

HAving thought it needful to warn you of the Mischiefs and Evils practised in the Sight of God by those called Freed Masons, I say take Care lest their Ceremonies and secret Swearings take hold of you; and be wary that none cause you to err from Godliness. For this devilish Sect of Men are Meeters in secret which swear against all without their Following. They are the Anti Christ which was to come leading Men from Fear of God. For how should Men meet in secret Places and with secret Signs taking Care that none observe them to do the Work of God; are not these the Ways of Evil-doers?

Knowing how that God observeth privilly them that Δt in Darkness they shall be smitten and the Secrets of their Hearts layed bare. Mingle not among this corrupt People lest you be found so at the World's Conflagration.

Set forth as a Warning to this Christian Generation by *H. Winter*, and Printed by *R. Sare* at Gray's Inn-gate, in *Holbourn*.

1698,

141
Freemasonry was being attacked on religious grounds even before it was formally organized. The above broadsheet was circulated in London in 1694.

all the religious and social orders introduced by Christianity, and building a new one according to its taste, based on the foundation and laws of naturalism'. He went on to warn of the Masonic intention of promoting democracy and secular education, from which 'universal revolution and subversion must come'—these being the aims of communists and socialists which are supported by Freemasonry 'because Masons promote their designs and have with them common capital principals'. Leo then argued that civil rulers should unite with the Church to oppose Freemasonry, reiterated all the Church's earlier prescriptions, and urged all members of the Catholic hierarchy to co-operate to 'root out this poison'. The encyclical ends with an exhortation to the Blessed Virgin Mary to aid the Church 'against the impious sects in which one sees clearly revived the contumacious pride, the untamed perfidy, the simulating shrewdness of Satan'. Publication of the encyclical let loose a torrent of partisan articles, pamphlets, and books, damning or praising the Craft according to the authors' allegiance. But among the many works condemning Freemasonry was a series by one man that would discomfit the Church to a degree it could scarcely have imagined.

At the time of the furore over *Humanum Genus*, Gabriel Jogand-Pages— Leo Taxil, to give him his better-known pseudonym—was well known for his scurrilous anti-clerical writing. A pamphlet of 1879, *Down with the Clergy*, led to a court case, although Taxil was acquitted; and the salacious *Secret Love Life of Pius IX* of 1881 brought not only another prosecution but also Taxil's expulsion from the Grand Orient, whose members were disgusted by the book, which they rightly perceived as going far beyond the bounds of decency. For all this, Taxil's anti-clerical career continued until 1885 when, to the chagrin of his own 'Anti-Clerical League', he suddenly announced his conversion and reconciliation with the Church. Now his literary talents were turned against his former friends, with the addition of a new target: Freemasonry. During 1886 alone he produced five exposures of and bitter attacks upon the Craft—presumably to the great satisfaction of Leo XIII, who granted Taxil the honour of a private audience in the following year. But still more startling revelations were yet to come.

In 1891 Taxil published *Are there Women in Freemasonry?* (*Y a-t-il des femmes dans la Franc-Maçonnerie?*), an expansion of an earlier work dealing with eighteenth-century Adoptive Masonry, brought up to date with references to what he called the 'New and Reformed Palladium', an androgynous rite allegedly directed from Charleston by Albert Pike, the Sovereign Grand Commander of the Scottish Rite. It was, claimed Taxil, an avowedly Satanic rite, imported into France by one Phileas Walder who founded the Mother-Lodge of the Lotus with the aid of disciples of the occultist Eliphas Lévi. Beyond the first three degrees are two virulently anti-Christian grades which involve the initiate in blasphemy, sacrilege, and—in the Templar-Mistress grade—ritualized sex (this to show 'that the sacred act of physical generation is the key to the mystery of being'). This absurd book was taken seriously by the Catholic hierarchy—Mgr. Fava, Bishop of Grenoble, praised it extravagantly; but his brains were already addled by notions of the Devil at work in Freemasonry—and led to a further wave of hysterical anti-Masonic works, including a fervent reaffirmation of Taxil's thesis by Adolphe Ricoux, a fantasist (to be kind) who printed what he said were 'Secret Instructions' to the Palladium from Albert Pike, whom he called 'Pope of the Freemasons'. It was all utter nonsense, no original documents were—or could be—produced, but the public swallowed it all. Albert Pike, said M. Ricoux, 'reformed the ancient Palladian Rite, and imparted thereto the Luciferian character in all its brutality'.

> Palladism, for him, is a selection; he surrenders to the ordinary lodges the adepts who confine themselves to materialism, or invoke the Grand Architect without daring to apply to him his true name, and under the title of Knights Templars and Mistress Templars, he groups the fanatics who do not shrink from the direct patronage of Lucifer.

As with Taxil, much of Ricoux's accompanying text is lifted *en bloc* (and unacknowledged) from the pages of Eliphas Lévi.

Taxil, however, was not to be outdone in his fervour. In 1893 he collaborated with Charles Hacks, a retired doctor of medicine, to produce a sensational work entitled *The Devil in the Nineteenth Century* by one 'Dr Bataille', who professed to have entered Palladism and seen all its wonders as he travelled around the world. Its High Priestess was now Sophie Walder, daughter of the founder of the Lotus Lodge, and the rite over which she ruled was truly amazing by any standards. Dr Bataille's revelations appeared in 240 parts, issued over the period of a year, during which readers were regaled with accounts of Satanic rituals, Masonic murders, the descent of Asmodeus bearing the Lion's tail of St Mark (lopped off during a battle between the angelic followers of Lucifer and Adonai), and—most delightful of all—the appearance at a Masonic *soirée* of a demonic crocodile who proceeded to sit down and play the piano.

All of this was accompanied by lurid illustrations, portraits of Luciferian Palladists interspersed with those of real, living Freemasons, and reproductions of both true and false Masonic documents. Despite all this the anti-Masons continued (for the most part) to believe such revelations; in *Humanum Genus* Leo XIII had demanded that the mask be torn from Freemasonry—here was its true face in all its black, satanic glory! and there was more to come.

Having disposed of Dr Bataille, Taxil turned to his most ingenious creation: a reformed and repentant ex-Palladist who would reveal in her

142 **Opposite**
A typical Taxil title page. His books were as noted for their lurid illustrations as for their scandalous contents.

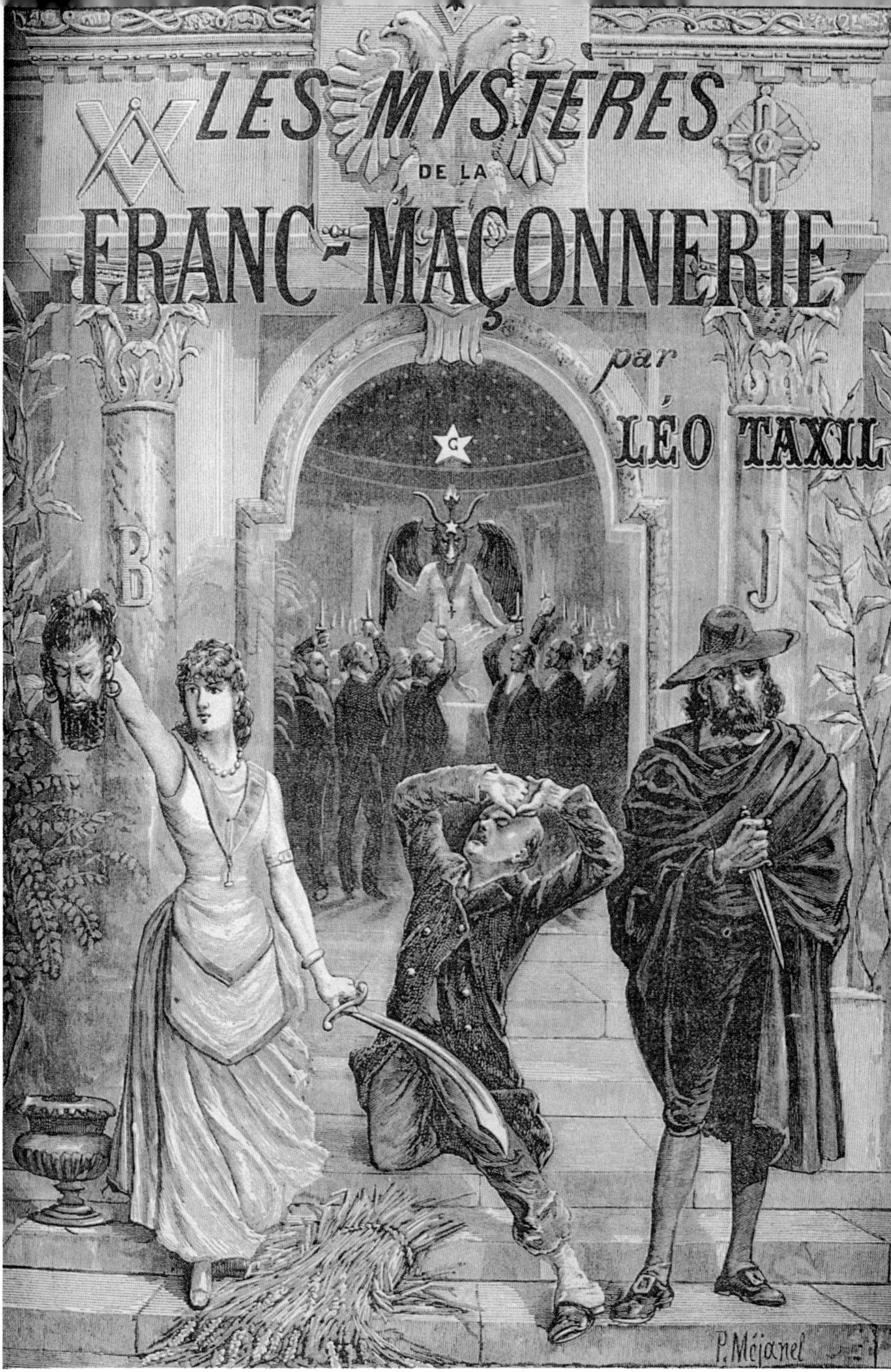
LES MYSTÈRES
DE LA
FRANC-MAÇONNERIE
par
LÉO TAXIL
G
B
J
P. Méjanel

143
William I, King of Prussia
1861, Emperor of Germany
1871-88. Protector of German
Freemasonry.

memoirs all the wickedness of Luciferian Freemasonry. On July 1895
Miss Diana Vaughan was born, appearing with the first of twenty-four
monthly numbers of her *Memoirs of an Ex-Palladist*. Control of the
Palladium—and of the Supreme Dogmatic Director of Universal
Freemasonry—had passed, on Albert Pike's death, to Adriano Lemmi, the
Italian Grand Master at Rome, or so Miss Vaughan claimed. She had
quarrelled with Sophie Walder and set up on her own 'Free and
Regenerated Palladium', but shortly after this came her conversion to

144
Emperor Frederick William 1st of Germany in the regalia of Master of a Lodge.

Rome (in another sense) and the first instalment of her memoirs. Descended from the union of Thomas Vaughan the alchemist and the goddess Astarte, Miss Vaughan had been dedicated as a Luciferian when sixteen years old and had spent much of her life since in dealings with devils; now she wished to expose their worshippers.

Among them she numbered Dr Westcott, the harmless head of the English Rosicrucian Society, and John Yarker, who controlled the Antient and Primitive Rite (a neat touch on Taxil's part, for the Rite of Memphis and Misraim was disliked by the Grand Orient). In this way Diana Vaughan surpassed Dr Bataille, for while she could not match his Satanic wonders she easily outdid him in libelling English Freemasons. They were not, however, without their defenders. A.E. Waite wrote a devastating *exposé* of the whole Palladium affair, demonstrating conclusively that it was a fiction pure and simple—an 'extraordinary literary swindle' in his own words—and he took justifiable pride in having 'unveiled the mass of fraud, falsehood and forgery contained in their depositions, and placed the position of the Roman Catholic Church in regard to the whole conspiracy in an unenviable light'.

By this time, 1896, many of the more rational members of the Church were becoming alarmed; the *Memoirs* were still appearing, Mgr. Fava still believed in a Satanic conspiracy, but demands were growing for Taxil to produce Diana Vaughan in the flesh. At the Anti-Masonic Congress of Trent, held in September 1896, open doubt was expressed as to her existence, but Taxil insisted that she be held in safety to avoid attempts on her life by furious Palladists. Somewhat mollified, the anti-Masons yet demanded a committee of enquiry to determine her true status, for 'Dr Bataille' had admitted that *his* work was a nonsense and thus, by implication, damned Miss Vaughan.

The final dénouement came on 19 April 1897 when Diana Vaughan was scheduled to appear in person at the lecture hall of the Geographical Society in Paris. In her place appeared Leo Taxil who explained in great detail how his elaborate hoax had been built up over twelve years; how his sole purpose had been to secure the discomfiture of the Roman Church; and how, although she was a real person, Diana Vaughan was simply his secretary and had no hand in producing her memoirs save to give them her name. 'The Palladium', said Taxil, 'exists no more. I was the creator of it, and I have destroyed it. You have nothing more to fear from its sinister influence.' Taxil then calmly left the platform and the hall, avoiding the ensuing pandemonium.

The embarrassment of the anti-Masons should have led to their downfall, but while Satanism was temporarily removed from the calendar of masonic crimes, anti-Masonry proceded on its venomous and bigoted way. One prominent French anti-Mason, M. Copin-Albancelli, argued in 1908 that Satanism still held sway in Masonic circles, albeit 'not in the sense that the devil comes to preside at their meetings, as that romancer of a Leo Taxil pretended, but in that their initiates profess the cult of Lucifer'. In these unspecified 'Masonic societies' the members repeat the formula 'Glory and Love for Lucifer! Hatred! Hatred! Hatred! to God, accursed, accursed, accursed!' As to proof of his claims, Copin-Albancelli stated that: 'I have read and studied hundreds of documents relating to one of these societies, documents that I have not permission to publish and which emanate from the members, men and women, of the group in question.' Which 'evidence' can lead only to the conviction that Copin-Albancelli was a liar of the first order.

The upheavals of the First World War, the political chaos that followed it, and the Russian Revolution all added fuel to the anti-Masonic fire. To the worship of Satan was now added the charge of a Judaeo-Masonic conspiracy aimed at overthrowing Christian civilization and promoting atheistic Communism. Those who propagated such views—and they were prominent in England as well as in France—built on older fancies of rabid anti-semites, some of whom were also anti-Masons; as, for example in Emil Eckert's *The Real Purpose of Freemasonry* (*Der Freimaurer-Orden in seiner wahren Bedeutung*, 1852) in which the author argued that the Jews and Masons were working together to destroy the existing, patriarchal social order.

Anti-semitic texts were not uncommon in the nineteenth century and all tended to propagate the image of the power-seeking, secretive, revolutionary Jew. The most infamous of such works appeared rather later, in Russia in 1905, and was brought to Western Europe after the Revolution by emigrés who blamed the Jews for their plight. The book in question was *The Protocols of the Learned Elders of Zion* by one Nilus, which purports to reveal a hidden scheme for the attainment of world domination by the Jews. It is, in fact, derived from a French satirical work of 1864, suitably doctored to inflame the anti-semitic passions of those who read and believed it. For anti-Masons it came as manna from heaven, for the Protocols state unequivocally: 'The Masonic Lodge (esoteric) throughout the world unconsciously acts as a mask for our purpose', which purpose was clearly 'the complete destruction of Christianity and the enslaving of all the Christian nations of the world under the heel of the Masonic Jews'—or so argued a particularly nauseous Irish anti-Mason, the Revd E. Cahill, a Jesuit professor of history who wilfully cast to the winds every normal canon of criticism when he produced his book *Freemasonry and the Anti-Christian Movement* (1929). Cahill argued that, whatever the truth about the *Protocols*, they represented true Jewish aims. He quotes a passage linking the 'Jewish Plot' with masonry:

Until the time when we attain power we will try to create and multiply lodges of Freemasons in all parts of the world . . . These lodges will be the principal places from which we shall obtain our information, as well as being centres of our propaganda. We will centralize these lodges under one management known to us alone, which will consist of our learned man.

For Cahill whatever the ultimate origin of the documents, and even if the *Protocols* in their present form were forgeries, they were yet 'based upon accurate knowledge of the Masonic conspiracy'.

145
Still from Forces Occultes, *a French anti-Masonic film produced under the Nazi domination of France.*

Such a repellent attitude was not commonly found in England, save in
the pseudo-scholarly conspiracy works of Nesta Webster (e.g. *Secret
Societies and Subversive Movements*, 1922) and the paranoid ravings of Miss
C.M. Stoddart (e.g. *Light-bearers of Darkness*, 1930). In France anti-
semitism and anti-Masonry were, alas, both more prevalent. The
unwholesome *Revue Internationale des Sociétés Secrètes* under the editorship
of that prince among bigots, Mgr. Jouin, spewed out its poison for many
years between the two World Wars while the scholar and esotericist René
Guenon encouraged anti-Masonic myths in many of his otherwise
eminently sane scholarly studies of esotericism. Worst of all was the quite
lunatic work of Lady Queenborough, author of the posthumous and quite
rabidly anti-Jewish *Occult Theocrasy* (1933). She managed to believe
implicitly every word of Leo Taxil's fictions, to see every social, political,
or religious society that might in any way be construed as promoting
democracy as an agent of the Jewish plot, and to see the whole conspiracy
as 'Jesuit-Judaic-Masonic-Gnostic-Brahmin-Illuminati' inspired. In view of
the eclecticism of her dislikes it is somewhat odd that she should
extravagantly praise the Italian Fascists.

And here is the essence of the wickedness of these rather silly anti-
Masons. Of themselves they are of little account; but they helped to
mould the attitudes of mind and thus the subsequent behaviour of
powerful figures in many of the repressive regimes that arose in Europe
after 1918. Russia had little need of their urgings, for far from being a
hotbed of revolutionary Masonic activity, the Soviet state ruthlessly
suppressed Freemasonry. At the Fourth Congress of the Communist
Internationale the following resolution was adopted:

It is absolutely necessary that the leading elements of the party should close all channels
which lead to the middle classes and should therefore bring about a definite breach with
Freemasonry. The chasm which divides the proletariat from the middle classes must be
clearly brought to the consciousness of the Communist Party. A small fraction of the
leading elements of the Party wished to bridge this chasm and to avail themselves of the
Masonic Lodges. Freemasonry is a most dishonest and infamous swindle of the
proletariat by the radically inclined section of the middle classes. We regard it our duty
to oppose it to the uttermost.

Right-wing regimes were equally hostile. In Italy, Mussolini and his
fascists attacked Freemasonry from the moment they came to power, first
requiring all Fascists to renounce Masonry, then attacking the Craft in
Fascist newspapers and so on to the physical destruction of Masonic
temples and their contents by Fascist thugs. Italian Masons maintained a
dignified stance, stressing their support for democracy and their
opposition to politically motivated violence; but despite appeals for
tolerance from Domizio Torrigiani, the Grand Master, anti-Masonic
violence continued. Following this, Torrigiani denounced Fascism as a

creed alien to Masonic ideals—with the consequence that an anti-Masonic law was passed in May 1925. Violence against persons and property continued, leading Torrigiani to order the cessation of all Masonic activity so that members should not suffer persecution. This, however, was of no avail. In November 1936 Torrigiani's deputy, General Capello, was arrested on a trumped-up charge and after a trial that was a travesty of justice sentenced to thirty years imprisonment. Immediately after the trial Torrigiani himself was arrested and banished, for 'agitation against the stage and government', to the Lipari Islands. So Freemasonry ceased in Italy until the downfall of Mussolini.

And as with Italy, so with Germany. The 'Judaeo-Masonic Conspiracy' theory was a convenient explanation for Germany's defeat in 1918, and it was propagated nowhere more vehemently than in General Ludendorff's immensely popular attack on Masonry, *The Extermination of Freemasonry by the Exposure of its Secrets* (1928). As might be expected from one so close to Hitler and so ardent a Nazi, the tenor of the book is vitriolically anti-Jewish: 'The secret of Freemasonry', wrote Ludendorff, 'is always the Jew!' This, of course, was nonsense for in Germany more than two-thirds of Freemasons were members of the Old Prussian lodges, which were exclusively Christian. In a far from creditable course of action, these lodges attempted to distance themselves from those that admitted Jews, but to no avail for the Nazi regime was determined to destroy *all* branches of Freemasonry. The Old Prussian Grand Lodges attempted to restructure themselves as 'German Christian Orders' and to remove all overtly Masonic elements from their working; but their fate was made clear in a speech of Dr Frick, the Minister of the Interior, who said, in August 1934:

It is inappropriate that a secret society with obscure aims should continue to exist in the Third Reich. It is high time that the Freemasons' lodges should disappear in Germany just as they have disappeared in Italy. If this is not realized in Masonic circles, I will soon help them in this direction.

Which he did: in May 1935 all the Grand Lodges were ordered to be dissolved, and Freemasonry disappeared throughout Germany. There followed an anti-Masonic campaign which led to savage persecution of Freemasons in countries occupied by the Nazis up to 1945. For those in Eastern Europe liberation brought no respite—Freemasonry is still forbidden in all countries under Communist rule.

The collapse of the dictatorships enabled the Craft to arise once more in both Germany and Italy; and as *their* dictators fell, so Freemasons could once again meet in Spain and Portugal. But even in nominally democratic countries the wind of hysterical anti-Masonry begins to blow again, for religious, political, and even social reasons. One argument, not heard in

146 Left
Elizabeth St. Leger (the Hon Mrs Aldworth) in her Masonic regalia.

147 Below
The idea of ladies accidentally discovering the 'secrets' of Freemasonry was popular with 18th century cartoonists. This is a typical example.

148 Above
*Meissen figure of a lady member
of the Order of Mopses, a quasi-
Masonic mixed Order popular
in the German princely Courts.
The pug dog had a repellant
part in the ritual.*

149 Right
*Annie Besant in her regalia as a
member of the Co-Masonic 33rd
degree.*

the past, is that the Craft is to be condemned because it refuses to admit women: and yet those women who seek to find Freemasonry *can* find it, after a fashion, in orders of their own.

In all his anti-Masonic works Leo Taxil stressed the horrors of androgynous Masonry, the lodges of which were seen as providing harems for male Freemasons, while the whole system led to nothing save the moral and physical degradation of women. But he also included a detailed account of the initiation into Masonry in 1882 of Maria Desraimes—an historical event that was, for once, not a figment of his imagination.

During the eighteenth century there had been several orders for women that paralleled Freemasonry (others, such as the Order of Mopses (pugdogs) in Germany, merely provided diversions for bored courtiers). Such orders were known as 'Adoptive' Masonry and their lodges were for both men and women. A system of three degrees—Apprentice, Fellow-Craft, and Mistress Mason—was worked, with legends and symbolism based on the Book of Genesis, and moral lessons drawn from the stories of Noah's Ark, Jacob's Ladder, and the Tower of Babel. They were, however, very much for dilettanti and did not survive the upheavals at the end of the century.

There had also been several instances of women gaining admission—by accident or design—to Masonic lodges and being summarily initiated. The most famous example is that of Mrs Aldworth who, as Elizabeth St Leger (Fig. 146), stumbled upon the lodge working in her father's house—Doneraile Court, in County Cork, Ireland—and was promptly made a Mason, taking the two degrees then extant (the affair took place about 1713—long before either the Grand Lodge of Ireland or the Master's Degree had come into being). For the rest of her life Mrs Aldworth saw herself as a true Mason and was treated as such; but the affair was an aberration—as were the few similar cases recorded in the eighteenth century. Wholesale admissions of women into Freemasonry did not take place for the simple reason that the Constitutions did not and do not permit it; nor were women greatly concerned about the fact until the 1880s, when the affair of Maria Desraimes brought the whole question to public notice.

When the Grand Independent Symbolic Lodge broke away from the Supreme Council of France, one of its subordinate lodges was *Les Libres Penseurs* at Le Pecq, a small town near Paris. In a fit of egalitarian passion the members of the lodge decided that Mlle. Maria Desraimes, an ardent feminist, should be admitted into Freemasonry, and the illicit initiation took place in January 1882. Mlle. Desraimes was subsequently passed and raised, but the Grand Lodge was outraged and at once suspended the Lodge of *Les Libres Penseurs*.

For ten years the lady remained in the Masonic wilderness until in 1893

150
A group of lady Co-Masons at Plymouth c.1920, wearing Mark and Scottish Rite regalia.

she was approached by Dr Georges Martin of the Supreme Council of France, himself an equally ardent feminist, with the suggestion that they establish a lodge for Masons of both sexes. Accordingly, in March and April 1893, Mlle. Desraimes initiated, passed, and raised sixteen female candidates who all became members of the new lodge, *Le Droit Humain* — the only lodge of the newly constituted *Grande Loge Symbolique Ecossaise Mixte de France*. Initially only the Craft degrees were worked, but as numbers increased so did the demand for higher degrees, and by 1900 a Supreme Council was established to govern the Order in its working of the degrees of the Ancient and Accepted Scottish Rite. More lodges were founded, the Theosophist Annie Besant (Fig. 149) was drawn in, and the order gained its most tireless worker.

In 1902 Mrs Besant brought mixed Masonry to Britain, established the lodge *Human Duty No. 6*, and promoted the Order within the Theosophical Society. Three years later she altered its title from 'Joint Freemasonry' to 'Universal Co-Freemasonry', which title it still retains, and took the post of 'Grand Master of the Supreme Council'; she could not be President as, after the death of Maria Desraimes in 1900, Georges Martin's wife took up that post. By 1908 the Order in Britain was experiencing its first schism: as a result of dissension over the Order's ritual, known as Dharma working and embodying many variations from standard Masonic practice, some members—both male and female—

broke away from Co-Freemasonry and founded the Honourable Fraternity of Ancient Masonry using rituals identical with those sanctioned by the United Grand Lodge of England. The Honourable Fraternity began as a mixed Order but now admits only women, and it has long eschewed the esoteric eccentricities of its Theosophical parent.

Co-Masonry has remained more willing to admit anyone and everyone, and has itself been tolerated by some of the irregular bodies in France. Georges Martin summed up its attitude and relationships in a speech of 1910:

We recognize all rites; we exclude none. If a Mason presents himself at the door of our temples, proving himself to be a Mason, we allow him to enter. In France, opinion is divided about us. The Grand Orient, up to now, permits its members to visit us but not to be affiliated to mixed lodges. The Rite Ecossais, however, not only allows its brethren to be affiliated to our Lodges, but even permits the Brothers of our Order to be 'regularized', affiliated that is, to the Rite Ecossais Lodges.

Such openness did not, however, prevent further schisms: in 1923 a considerable number of members broke away to form the Antient and Honourable Fraternity of Freemasonry for Men and Women, surviving to the present day as a small but active body.

Regular Masonry, however, does not recognize either mixed orders or those that admit only women; its reasons are simple—women are barred from Freemasonry by the Ancient Landmarks that permit only men to be initiated. It is unlikely in the extreme that this position will change in the foreseeable future. Most Masons would probably not wish for any change and would echo the sentiments of John Coustos, who in 1743 told the Portuguese Inquisition:

That the reason why Women were excluded from the Society, was, to take away all occasion of calumny and reproach, which would have been unavoidable, had they been admitted into it. Further, that since women had, in general, been always considered as not very well qualified to keep a secret; the founders of the Society of Free-Masons, by their exclusion of the other sex, thereby gave a signal proof of their prudence and wisdom.

7
Freemasonry in America

THROUGHOUT the period of its growth in the American colonies Freemasonry was effectively free from public attack, principally because the major sources of anti-Masonry were absent: the colonies were not subject to papal authority and the politically motivated quasi-Masonic orders had not yet come into being. Public tolerance of the Craft as a respectable and beneficent social institution continued throughout the revolutionary period, when Freemasons were to be found actively involved in the struggle amongst both rebels and loyalists. Indeed, it was not until the appearance of an American edition of Robison's *Proofs of a Conspiracy* in 1798 that specific attacks upon the Craft began to occur.

After reading the book, and becoming affected by its hysterical style, a New England clergyman, the Revd Jedidiah Morse, preached a sermon based on Robison's thesis that Freemasonry was subversive. The sermon was widely reprinted and used extensively and uncritically by ministers, of all denominations, who were hostile to the Craft. Sermons in defence of Freemasonry were also delivered, but the mischief had been done and the foundations laid for organized religious anti-Masonry which slowly gathered strength. By the early 1820s both the Presbyterian and Methodist Churches in Pennsylvania—and they were not the only examples—had condemned Masonry, but the real storm did not break until 1826, and when it did it had decidedly political as well as religious overtones.

In 1826 American society was in a state of flux. The country was gradually emerging from a long period of economic depression—brought about by the Napoleonic wars and the war with Britain from 1812 to

No. 7.

THE NEW-ENGLAND
ANTI-MASONIC ALMANAC
FOR THE YEAR OF OUR LORD
1835.

"THE VOICE OF MORGAN'S BLOOD CRIES FROM THE GROUND."

FREEMEN "SCORN TO BE SLAVES."

MASONIC MORTAR.

1. *How-ard*, to detect a Masonic murderer. By Masonic aid escaped to Europe.
2. The *Butcher* escaped to Canada, and was killed by a fall from his horse. Divine justice stronger than human.
3. A Masonic Grand King, died suddenly before his trial, after Bruce disclosed.
4. Personification of Masonry, persisting in cementing the walls of its temple in *human blood*.

·BOSTON:·
Published and sold by JOHN MARSH, Proprietor of the copyright, No. 84 Washington street—Jones and Oakes, State street, Boston.

Sold also by I. Wilcox, Providence, R. I.; B. D. Packard, & Co. Albany, N. Y.; L. D. Dewey & Co., and David Felt, New York; N. Eggleston, Hartford, Ct.; Colman, Holden, & Co., Portland, and office of the Free Press, Hallowell, Me.; Dorr, Howland & Co. Worcester, Mass. and Booksellers generally.

151 **Left**
The growth of anti-Masonry led to the publication of anti-Masonic almanacs. This version ran from 1828 to the early 1840s.

152 **Below**
The Gothic inspired Masonic Hall on Broadway, New York, 1830.

1814—but conflicts over the political structure and complexion of the nation still continued. Increasing immigration from Europe permitted a successful westward expansion into virgin territory rich in the resources needed for both agriculture and industry, but tensions—moral as well as economic—arose between rural communities rooted in the narrow Puritan ethic and cities that were perceived (and self-perceived) as being both more open and more sophisticated. And accompanying all this was the dawn of an era of religious change: the decades to come would see innumerable local religious 'revivals' and the rise of a bewildering variety of new and bizarre sects and cults, such as the Mormonism of Joseph Smith. Given such fertile soil it is not surprising that the seeds of anti-Masonry, once sown, would rapidly germinate. They were finally sown in full measure, in the shape of one William Morgan, at Batavia in Western New York State.

From an objective viewpoint, William Morgan does not appear to have been an attractive personality. He was an itinerant bricklayer, born in 1774 at Culpepper in Virginia. In 1819 he married and soon after migrated to Canada to work in a brewery, returning to the USA in 1823 and settling at Batavia. Here he followed his trade in a somewhat indolent manner, spending more time in drinking and in spinning yarns (he claimed—falsely, for the stories are not borne out by contemporary military records—to have fought in the war of 1812 and to have been given the rank of captain) than in working. His drinking habits led him into debt (he was sued by his creditors on four occasions in 1826 alone) and they were not disputed, even by his supporters: one prominent anti-Mason, Samuel Greene, wrote that Morgan was, 'a convivial man, and at times would drink freely, according to the fashions of the day. I myself have seen him when he had been drinking more than was good for him, but he was not what, in the general acceptation of the word at that time, or at any time, would be called a drunkard.'

Greene, presumably stung by comments that Morgan had been 'a sot', 'a rum soak', and 'a hanger-on at grog shops', and speaking as a former Mason, further remarked, somewhat tartly, that, 'It was the period of hard and general drinking, and certainly it ill becomes Freemasons to charge men on this score, for no body of men among us have done more, from generation to generation, to promote drinking habits than they.'

That Morgan was also a romancer also seems certain, and the Masonic writer Rob Morris stated flatly: 'The most credulous man in the village would have scorned to believe anything William Morgan said, unless corroborative evidence could be had.' None the less, the Freemasons of Batavia accepted Morgan as one of their brethren when he claimed to have been made a Mason in Canada, although no evidence has ever been forthcoming that he was initiated in Canada, in the USA, or anywhere else.

153
Masonic charts were even more popular in America than Britain. This typical example dates from the 1840s.

Whatever the truth of his Masonic membership, Morgan was accepted locally and in 1825 was exalted in a local Royal Arch chapter. He evidently familiarized himself with Masonic ritual and developed an impressive style of working the ceremonies; but whether from doubts about his Masonic regularity or from unease at his social behaviour, his brethren in Batavia declined to permit his involvement in a newly chartered chapter within the town.

As a consequence of this rejection—or, as seems more likely, as a means of raising money and escaping from his creditors—Morgan determined to write an exposure of the Masonic ceremonies. The projected book, provisionally entitled *Illustrations of Masonry by one of the Fraternity. God said let there be light and there was light*, was to be printed by a local newspaper publisher, David C. Miller, who hoped to profit substantially from it (he, too, was in financial difficulties). As news of the impending publication spread, so feelings among local Masons ran high and instead of pursuing the sensible course of saying and doing nothing, and thus permitting the book to fall stillborn from the press, they threatened Miller

154
An American folk hero and Freemason who spanned the great period of both national and Masonic developments.

155
The portrait shows the typical dress of a mid-19th century American Grand Master.

with violence if he did not drop the project (or so he claimed in the August issue of his *Republican Advocate*) and there were two apparent attempts to burn down his newspaper office.

The next episode in the saga was Morgan's arrest, on a charge of petty theft, on 11 September 1826. He was taken to Canadaigua (where the theft allegedly took place) some fifty miles away, where he was examined but acquitted of the charge—only to be immediately re-arrested and jailed for non-payment of a trifling debt. On the following day he was released and taken, evidently against his will, in a coach to Fort Niagara where he was detained in a disused powder magazine. No further trace of Morgan was ever found and rumours began to circulate that he had been murdered by the Masons. The excitement following these rumours led to a series of anti-Masonic meetings at Batavia and to three proclamations from the Governor of New York (De Witt Clinton, himself a Mason) urging the utmost efforts to apprehend the abductors of Morgan and offering a substantial reward of $1,000 together with a free pardon to anyone who 'as accomplice or co-operator shall make a full discovery of the offender or offenders'.

There was, of course, no charge of murder for there was no body, but in October 1827 the discovery of a body of a drowned man some forty miles from Niagara renewed the excitement. An initial verdict of accidental death at the inquest brought an outcry, a successful demand for an exhumation, and a second inquest at which Morgan's widow identified the body as that of her husband. Unfortunately for the anti-Masonic faction, the publicity over the two inquests brought a Mrs Sarah Monro from Newcastle in Canada, who identified the corpse—with minute descriptions of both the body and clothing—as that of *her* husband, Timothy Monro, who had been drowned on 24 September 1827 while returning from the American shore in a rowing boat. It should be noted that the corpse was apparently bearded while Morgan was clean shaven and balding (indeed, in the portrait engraving in his posthumous book he appears as the epitome of a benign Mr Pickwick). This, however, made no difference to the anti-Masonic faction, who had now established a political platform and argued that the body 'is a good enough Morgan until after the election!'

Murder could thus still not be shown, but those who had abducted Morgan were punished severely. Three of them, all Masons, who had been members of the party that arrested Morgan were gaoled, as was Eli Bruce, the Sheriff of Niagara County who had helped to arrange the last coach ride and had ridden in the coach with Morgan. A fifth conspirator, John Whitney, was later alleged to have admitted on his deathbed to his part in a supposititious murder, but the circumstantial details did not fit and Whitney's son-in-law strenuously denied that such a confession took place. Instead, Whitney is supposed to have bribed Morgan to disappear in Canada with $500 in his pocket—the abduction and confinement were due to lack of trust on Whitney's part—but the alleged signed statement of Morgan promising not to return has never been seen. Since the time of his disappearance there have been more than a dozen alleged explanations of Morgan's fate but only one appears to ring true.

According to this story Morgan sailed from Canada, became shipwrecked on the vessel *Constance*, but was rescued and taken to the Cayman Islands. Here he settled, married in 1829, had nine children, and finally died in 1864 at the age of 89. This age corresponds with that of *the* William Morgan and as the Cayman Morgan was supposed to have been buried with Masonic regalia and was rumoured to have given away Masonic secrets, it seems at least probable that he was the William Morgan from Batavia. What does not seem to have been considered is that David Miller may well have had a hand in Morgan's disappearance—the furore over the supposed 'murder' vastly increased sales of the book and would have netted a small fortune for Miller had he not suffered from the many unauthorized editions issued by publishing pirates. That, at least, can be seen as poetic justice.

Morgan's book eventually appeared in November 1826 and ran into innumerable editions, being continually enlarged and later appropriated by other authors. The most important expansion of his book was Elder David Bernard's *Light on Masonry* (1829), which included not only the rituals of the Craft Degrees but also those of the entire sequence of the Ancient and Accepted Scottish Rite—the publication of which was one of the factors leading to Albert Pike's reconstruction of the Scottish Rite ceremonies. In addition Bernard printed a complete account of the Morgan affair, with an appendix of documents, and reports of the proceedings of the various subsequent anti-Masonic gatherings throughout New York State. These were merely the first of many.

Anti-Masonic conventions were held throughout 1827, but the first of any significance was a convention of Baptist Churches, held at Milton, New York, in September 1827, at which fifteen reasons were given for denouncing and opposing Freemasonry. Of these fifteen, all save two are religious in character, accusing Freemasonry of being irreligious, unscriptural, syncretistic, pagan ('its rites correspond with the Egyptian'), and not specifically Christian. The arguments are also tinged with bigotry, showing anti-semitism ('it authorizes prayers accommodated to the prejudices of the Jews') and anti-Catholicism ('it adopts orders of Knighthood from Popery'). One argument is surprising for the time: the order is condemned 'because it excludes the female sex'. Given contemporary attitudes to female emancipation, this can only have been included as a subtle means of encouraging wives to persuade their

156 Opposite
The Gothic inspired Masonic Hall, Philadelphia 1855-73.

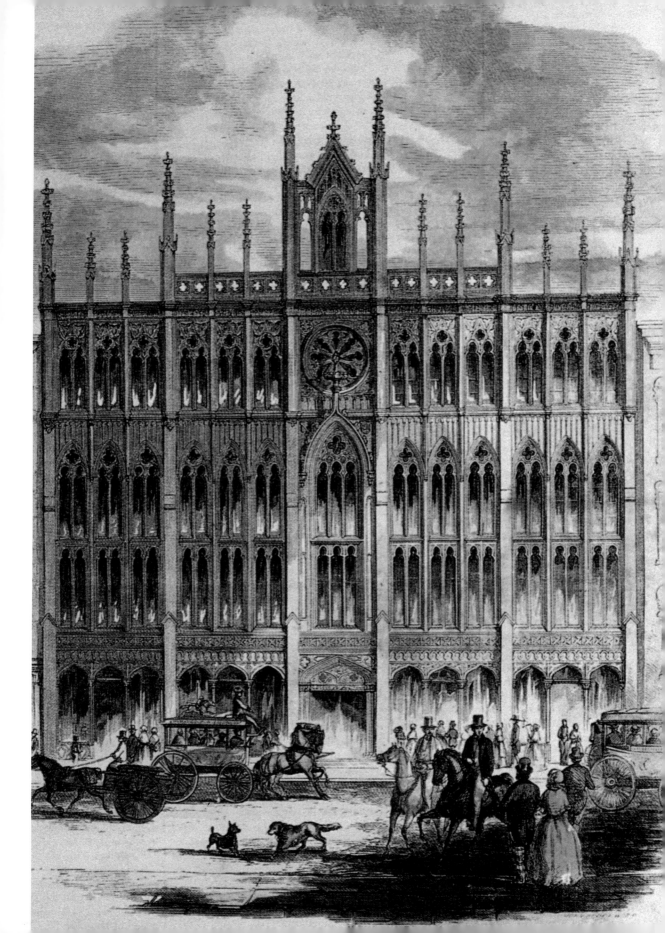

157 Right
Watercolour of the present Masonic Hall, Philadelphia, built in 1873.

158 Below
The Lodge Rooms in Philadelphia all commemorate a particular architectural style. This is the Norman Room.

husbands to leave the Craft.

An earlier, non-denominational convention had condemned Masonry for being anti-social, undemocratic, a corrupting influence, and an encouragement to 'the commission of crime by affording the means of escape'. Accusations were made that Masonry led to idleness, intemperance, dissipation, criminality, and also self-righteousness! That this last was equally true of the anti-Masons did not occur to them. Freemasons themselves responded vigorously, as might have been expected: the abduction of Morgan was condemned, and the Grand Lodge of Vermont issued an address in which involvement in the Morgan affair was denied and the following points emphasized:

Masons, above all men, must obey the laws of God and Men. Their solemn obligations require a strict obedience of those laws. So far from binding him to any engagement inconsistent with the happiness, prosperity and welfare of the nation, these obligations doubly require him to be true to his God, his country and his fellow men. In the language of the ancient Constitution of the Order, which is in print and open to be inspected by all men, he is charged 'to keep and obey the moral law; to be a quiet and peaceable citizen, true to his government and just to his country'.

But such statements were to no avail. The anti-Masonic movement had the bit between its teeth and anti-Masonic feeling was rapidly whipped-up throughout New England and the north-eastern states. From being a series of local crusades against Masonry the movement developed into a political party with a specific platform of opposing the election of Masons to public office and of working towards the general suppression of Freemasonry. As with all 'third parties', the anti-Masonic element acted more as a catalyst for disaffected supporters of both the Democratic and National Republican parties, but the hysteria engendered by the Morgan affair brought the new party a surprising degree of support in New York, Pennsylvania, and throughout New England. Its success in New York, where fifteen anti-Masonic candidates were elected to the State legislature in 1827, was largely due to the organizing genius of Thurlow Weed, a prominent journalist and political boss who worked tirelessly promoting anti-Masonry (in which he genuinely believed) and opposing the 'Albany Regency' of Martin Van Buren and his Democrats. But bitter conflicts arose among some anti-Masons over their divided loyalties and by dividing the anti-Democrat vote they succeeded in the election for state Governor in 1828 merely in ensuring the re-election of Van Buren on a minority vote.

In his *Autobiography*, published in 1882, Weed described the bitterness of the elections at that time:

The feelings of the Masons, exasperated by the existence of a political organization which made war upon the institution of Freemasonry, became intensely so by the renunciation of Masonry by ministers, elders and deacons of the Presbyterian, Methodist and Baptist

Churches. The conflict therefore became more embittered and relentless, personally, politically, socially and ecclesiastically, than any other I have ever participated in, and more so probably than any ever known in our country. Thousands of Masons, innocent of any wrong and intending to remain neutral, were drawn into the conflict, when all were denounced who adhered to the institution. On the other hand, the anti-Masons maintained that the abduction and murder of Morgan resulted legitimately from the obligations and teachings of the Order.

Feelings ran equally high in other States. Anti-Masonry gathered strength in Pennsylvania from the Quakers and the many German Protestant sects who condemned the taking of oaths, and by 1829 the anti-Masonic party had one Congressman, one State Senator, and fifteen Assemblymen. But the party was weakened by the great variety of conflicting local interests in Pennsylvania, which invariably took precedence in the voting behaviour of its members in the legislature. Even so, in the 1832 election for governor, Joseph Ritner, the anti-Masonic candidate, was only narrowly defeated while in 1835 he obtained the governorship with a substantial majority of the votes. His election had been aided by the efforts of Thaddeus Stevens, an outstanding state politician and virulent anti-Mason, who had endeavoured to bring forward a series of bills attacking Masonry. All had failed, or had been heavily amended, but with Ritner as Governor an act was passed 'To suppress secret societies bound together by unlawful oaths'. A committee was set up, with Stevens as chairman, to 'investigate the evils of Freemasonry', but the Masons called before it simply refused to testify and protested against the act so that it gradually withered away, taking with it the anti-Masonic party that had created it.

New England also suffered from the anti-Masonic hysteria, fostered by the Puritanical spirit that prevailed in rural areas; but it was only in one state—Vermont—that the anti-Masonic party achieved any real success. In 1831 an anti-Masonic Governor, William Palmer, was elected; an act was passed forbidding extra-judicial oaths; and Masons were so cowed that the Grand Lodge of Vermont ceased to hold sessions for more than fifteen years and every lodge in the state either surrendered its warrant or became dormant. This, indeed, was the most pernicious effect of the anti-Masonic moral blackmail: men were afraid to admit to masonic membership for fear that persecution by anti-Masonic bigots would ruin their businesses and deprive them of their livelihoods.

During the period of political anti-Masonry the decline in the Craft was marked in the North-East; in New York State membership declined from 20,000 to 3,000 between 1825 and 1835 while the number of lodges fell from 480 to 75 (of which only 50 were active); numbers also fell dramatically in New Jersey and Massachusetts, while even states that resisted anti-Masonry (Ohio and Pennsylvania) saw a drop in membership.

The high-water mark of anti-Masonry was, however, fast approaching and its nemesis was soon to follow. In September 1830 an anti-Masonic convention at Baltimore nominated William Wirt of Maryland as the party's candidate in the presidential election of 1832. Wirt was not an especially active anti-Mason, having told the convention that 'I have thought and repeatedly said that I consider Masonry as having nothing to do with politics, and nothing has surprised me more than to see it blown into consequence.' Perhaps as a counterbalance to this, his partner as vice-presidential candidate, Amos Ellmaker, was noted for his virulent hatred of the Craft. Inevitably, Wirt was crushingly defeated: Andrew Jackson gained 219 electoral votes against Henry Clay's 49, while Wirt obtained only the 7 votes from Vermont—the most extreme of anti-Masonic state legislatures. After this defeat the party gradually declined—except in Pennsylvania, where it was active throughout the mid-1830s. Nationally it tended to act in collaboration with the National Republicans and in 1836 united with them to form the Whig Party until the efforts of Thurlow Weed, who was also prominent in the anti-slavery movement, brought them in 1856 under the umbrella of the Republican Party.

One would have hoped that anti-Masonic bigotry had died with the party, but this, alas, did not happen. The anonymous author of a catalogue of anti-Masonic books issued in 1852 prefixed his account of the distribution of anti-Masonic literature throughout America with a scurrilous and baseless list of 'deaths and sudden disappearances' that can 'now be pretty satisfactorily accounted for by the probable infliction of the *Masonic penalty*'. Fifteen years later a group of clergymen met at Aurora, Illinois to discuss the organization of a national convention on 'secret societies', following up their discussion with the founding in May 1868 of the 'National Association of Christians opposed to Secret Societies'. This body was chartered in 1874 as the National Christian Association with headquarters in Chicago, from which it still operates its decidedly un-Christian activities against Freemasonry. Its principal activity was, and is, the publication of a monthly magazine, the *Christian Cynosure*, devoted to vicious attacks upon the Craft.

The National Christian Association is also opposed, *inter alia*, to Jesuitism and Mormonism—both of which are hostile to Freemasonry—and it is odd to find the *Christian Cynosure* cited extensively in the *Dictionary of Secret and other Societies* (1924) by the Roman Catholic anti-Mason, Arthur Preuss. Even more odd is the same volume's omission of any account of the Roman Catholic Order of the Knights of Columbus, an avowedly sectarian order founded in 1882 with rituals that plagiarize those of Freemasonry. In 1949 the same Order issued a booklet, *Why the Catholic Church says 'Investigate'*, which includes in its text an attack upon the Craft. More recent Roman Catholic attacks have, however, been less

159 **Right**
*An artist's impression of the
Masonic Hall in Chicago, the
tallest building in 1880s
Chicago.*

160 **Below**
*Albert Pike 1809-91.
Conservator of the Scottish Rite
in the southern jurisdiction of
the USA.*

vitriolic than in the past and the present position of the papal authorities *vis à vis* Freemasonry has become somewhat more accommodating.

This is not the case with Mormonism, the religious sect founded in 1830 by Joseph Smith on the basis of the gold plates allegedly discovered at Palmyra in New York State in 1827. By 1839 the Mormons had been driven out of their settlement in Missouri and moved to a site in Illinois that they named Nauvoo. Immediately, those of them who were Masons petitioned the Grand Lodge of Illinois for the founding of a lodge at Nauvoo. Despite local Masonic opposition, a lodge was established under dispensation in 1842, but its irregular activities—and those of other newly formed Mormon lodges—led within two years to the Grand Lodge of Illinois revoking their dispensations. The Nauvoo lodges, however, ignored the Grand Lodge instructions and went their own way until they came to an end after the murder of Joseph Smith in June 1844.

Smith himself had been made a Mason at the first meeting of the Nauvoo Lodge and proceeded to utilize Masonic ceremonies in the inner rituals of his own sect. After his death the process was evidently continued for the Obligations and other parts of the temple ceremonies as used at Nauvoo in 1846 are taken almost directly from the rituals of the Craft degrees. This is explained by Mormon apologists as being due to Joseph Smith having received a revelation of the true temple ceremonies of which Masonic rituals are but imperfect examples. Many of the symbols carved on the temple at Salt Lake City are also Masonic in their more common usage—unless one is disposed to be charitable and to refer them to their ultimate biblical source and to explain by coincidence the mutual combinations of the same symbols.

In more recent years, whether from religious fervour, or from embarrassment at the obvious Masonic origin of their ceremonies is not at all clear, the Mormon authorities have prohibited their members from becoming Masons, arguing that Masonry originated with Satan and must thus be avoided! Thus Mormonism perpetuates and practises anti-Masonry—perhaps the only body to do so for reasons of self-preservation.

Current manifestations of American anti-Masonry are to be found, however, not so much among obscure sects as among ultra-conservative fundamentalist 'Christians' who justify their hostility to a considerable degree by reference to the Masonic writings of the most famous American Freemason of the last century: Albert Pike (Fig. 160). More specifically, they cite his best known work, *Morals and Dogma of the Ancient and Accepted Scottish Rite of Freemasonry*, a copy of which is still required reading for every new member of the Rite. Given Pike's highly idiosyncratic opinions and the fact that, when asked by an evangelical group which were the most authoritative Masonic books, more than half of the Grand Lodges of the United states cited *Morals and Dogma*, it is not surprising that anti-Masons use the book—with some justice—as a basis for their attacks. What, save hostility, can be expected when the fundamentalist is faced with such passages as these?

Masonry is a *worship* . . . the universal, eternal, immutable religion, such as God planted it in the heart of universal humanity . . . The Ministers of this religion are all Masons who comprehend it and are devoted to it . . .

The God of . . . the Christian world is only Bel, Moloch, Zeus, or at best Osiris, Mithras or Adonai, under another name . . .

They are, of course, taken out of context and to understand them one must not only set them in place but also bear in mind what Pike sought to achieve, and consider to what degree he attained his goals.

Albert Pike was a man of many and diverse talents, and gifted with an outstanding intellect—albeit marred by a lack of academic discipline and fine critical judgement, consequent upon the abrupt curtailment (for financial reasons) of his formal education after one year at Harvard. He was born in 1809 in Boston, but left New England at the age of 21 and travelled through the then little-known south-western states, eventually settling at Little Rock in Arkansas, where he married, taught himself law, and built a highly successful legal practice for himself. He had already turned his hand to journalism and now went on to publish both poetry and legal works, in addition to raising a large family and taking up the Masonic pursuits that were eventually to become the focus of his life. In 1861 his career took a new turn when he was appointed by the Confederacy as an agent to deal with the Indians of Oklahoma and northern Texas. Pike was then commissioned brigadier-general to command the Indian territory where he had effected treaties with all the tribes; but he argued against their taking part in the Civil War outside their own territory and eventually resigned his command (although he did command the Indians, under protest, at the Battle of Pea Ridge in Missouri; an action that led to his indictment on a charge of inciting the Indians against the government). After the war he received a pardon, moved to Memphis, and then, in 1868, to Washington where he continued his legal practice and remained for the rest of his life.

Pike was initiated into Freemasonry at Little Rock in 1850 and by 1854 he was the Master of Magnolia Lodge, which he had helped to found two years before. In 1853 he had transferred his legal practice to New Orleans and it was there that he learned of the Ancient and Accepted Scottish Rite. He received all of its degrees from the 4th to the 32nd in March of that year at Charleston, South Carolina, and in 1857 received the 33rd degree. But he was profoundly dissatisfied with the ceremonies of each degree, and expressing his dissatisfaction he was appointed to a committee set up to reconstruct the rituals. This revision—effectively a complete rewriting—took place over thirteen years from 1855 to 1868 and was the work of Pike alone. Nor was this all, for he also produced a liturgy for each degree and a series of instructional lectures that were published in 1871 as *Morals and Dogma*. His work did not go unrecognized—indeed it could not, for it moulded the very structure of the Scottish Rite—and in 1859 he was elected Grand Commander of the Supreme Council (Southern Jurisdiction), which pre-eminent office he held until his death in 1891. But what was the Rite, and what were the rituals on which Pike exercised so powerful an influence?

As we have seen in Chapter 2, the Ancient and Accepted Scottish Rite developed out of the Rite of Perfection of 25 Degrees, which itself originated in the bewildering mass of *Hauts Grades* that had proliferated in France from 1740 onwards. In 1767 a Lodge of Perfection was founded at Albany in New York by Henry Francken, who had brought the Rite from Jamaica, and from there it spread in a desultory fashion down the eastern seaboard, with little certain knowledge surviving as to how it developed. All that *is* certain is that in 1801 the 'Mother Supreme Council 33° Ancient and Accepted Scottish Rite' was formed at Charleston by John Mitchell, Frederick Dalcho, and seven others, all claiming to work on the

161
The Scottish Rite building in Dallas, Texas. Like most American Masonic buildings at the turn of the 20th century it is severely classical in style.

"I dearly love a MASON, because-
a Mason's "ON THE SQUARE"!"

basis of Constitutions of 1786 (whose true status and exact date are by no means clear) which transformed the Rite of Perfection of 25 Degrees to the thirty-three degree Scottish Rite.

From that time on the history of the Scottish Rite in America is one of increasing complexity and, in the northern states, of virtual chaos; it is a tale of division, rivalries, and schisms; of irregular bodies and spurious Supreme Councils (one of which, based on the bodies founded by Joseph Cerneau from 1807 onwards, survived until 1919). In the 1820s and 1830s the Scottish Rite was affected by the anti-Masonry that was threatening the Craft degrees, but as the tide of hostility retreated so that Rite spread through the southern states—not that it was prominent in its early days: Albert Pike had not heard of it until 1853—and gradually attained its

present prominent place in Masonic activities. After the end of the Civil War in 1865 attempts were made to bring order to the Rite in the northern states.

There were supposedly only two Supreme Councils in North America, but that in the north remained fragmented until all the warring bodies were finally merged in 1867. The Rite has become as popular in the north as in the south, taking as it does virtually all the additional degrees under its wing. It is the strict control that has permitted those who seek them to find a variety of rituals within one rite and had prevented the influx of any rites which have a revolutionary, political basis—and by so doing it has also prevented any modern manifestation of the anti-Masonic hysteria of the 1820s. But the price has been the acceptance of Pike's rituals and of his

163
Officers of the Boumi Temple of the Ancient Arabic Order, Nobles of the Mystic Shrine, Baltimore, 1904.

curious philosophical analysis of their meaning.

Most of those who enter the Scottish Rite probably do so for social reasons; but for those who seek spiritual and philosophical meanings above and beyond the moral precepts of the Craft degrees, Pike's rituals provide them in abundance. They are unlike the Ancient and Accepted Rite in Great Britain, which is wholly Christian, being entirely unsectarian since Pike wished the Rite to be open to men of all faiths without any specific judgements being made upon their beliefs. It is this very universalism that enrages anti-Masonic Christians who cannot understand what Pike was attempting to do.

The rituals as Pike found them 'were a heterogenous and chaotic mass, in many parts of incoherent nonsense and jargon, in others of jejuneness; in some of the degrees of absolute nothingness'. He became convinced that 'their real meaning had originally been communicated orally and that the Rituals were purposely so framed to mislead those into whose hands they might unlawfully fall'. This was his opinion in 1861 when he was busy with the rewriting; by the time he had finished his task he would say instead (in 1878): 'The Truth is that the Rite was nothing, and the Rituals almost naught, for the most part a lot of worthless trash, until 1855.' And towards the end of his life, in 1887, he gave his final judgement upon the old rituals: 'They were trivial, insipid, without originality, contemptible as literary productions, mere collections of flat, dull, common-place.' This assessment would meet with the approval of most modern critics, who can read the texts of the old rituals in Bernard's *Light on Masonry* (1829) and see for themselves how uninspired and inconsequential they are. Pike's rituals are, by contrast, colourful, dramatic and well-structured, however syncretistic they may be. His principal failings—which are clearly visible in *Morals and Dogma*—are an inability to treat comparative religion in an objective manner and an overriding conviction that all belief systems, however incompatible they may be one with another, are somehow reducible to a common denominator within Freemasonry. And yet it was all done in the name of tolerance: Pike sought to be even-handed with men of all religions, and thus, buried within seas of bizarre speculations, one finds islands of clear and simple common sense:

We teach the truth of none of the legends we recite. They are to us but parables and allegories, involving and enveloping Masonic instruction; and vehicles of useful and interesting information.

It is this openness, this tolerance of and sympathy towards all men that is Pike's legacy. More even than the coherent and sound institution that has grown from his organizing genius, it is the spirit within the Scottish Rite that has made it what it is today.

Once the trauma of the Morgan incident had been worked through,

164
Prince Hall's application to England for a Warrant for a lodge.

165
The Warrant for African Lodge.

American Freemasonry grew tremendously. With the exception of fundamentalist sniping it has been remarkably free from the slur of anti-Masonry. This is possibly for two reasons. First, American Freemasonry, like many other American organizations, has always had a very high public profile. Masonic buildings, particularly those of the Scottish Rite, are not only imposing but their function is obvious and well known. Public processions and ceremonials, particularly the Shriners carnival-like processions, mean that the local population are in no doubt as to whom the local Freemasons are. Second, in this century, American Freemasons have done a great deal in the area of public charity.

Many of the State Grand Lodges support homes for elderly Freemasons and their widows and orphaned or disadvantaged children of Freemasons. Most of the Grand Lodges and other Masonic organizations have scholarship funds that provide money for higher education and vocational training regardless of whether or not the recipients have any Masonic connections. Outside its own circle Freemasonry in the United States has done a great deal to promote research and treatment of illness in and accidents to children. Both Jurisdictions of the Scottish Rite and the Shriners (Ancient Arabic Order of the Nobles of the Mystic Shrine) have built and supported children's hospitals, burns units, and clinics dealing with language disorders. In addition to treating *any* sick children, these facilities have also taken on extensive research programmes that have greatly extended the medical world's knowledge and treatment of children's illnesses and accidents. In addition, Freemasonry has funded research into the problems of cancer, schizophrenia, and the present scourges of alcohol and drug abuse. In 1985, the last year for which figures are available, Masonic organizations in the USA provided over 300 million dollars to support projects within the community as a whole (Figs. 164-6).

Running parallel with regular Freemasonry in the USA, and other parts of the world, is Prince Hall Masonry, which for historical reasons is not accepted as regular. Much has been written of the life and Masonic career of Prince Hall, most of it inaccurate. His origins are unknown, despite many colourful biographies. The earliest record of him is his Certificate of Manumission dated 9 April 1770. In 1775 he and other coloured men were made Freemasons, reputedly in an Irish military lodge stationed in Boston, Massachusetts. They apparently received a permit from John Rowe, Provincial Grand Master (English) for North America, to walk in procession on St John's day and appear to have used it as a dispensation to hold a lodge. In 1784 they applied to the premier Grand Lodge in England for a warrant as a regular lodge and were granted No. 459 as African Lodge, Boston, on 29 September 1784. Thereafter the African Lodge functioned as a normal lodge until contact was lost with the Grand Lodge in England *c.*1800, possibly due to bad communications as a result

166
A 19th century artist's impression of Prince Hall. It is remarkably similar to a popular engraving of Thomas Smith Webb, the white American author of Masonic manuals and ritual guides.

of the Napoleonic Wars. Despite the loss of contact African Lodge was kept on the English register until 1814 when it, and all the other American lodges, was removed at the sort out of the registers after the union.

Thus far there is no problem. In 1797, however, a number of coloured Masons in Philadelphia wrote to Prince Hall for authority to meet as a lodge. This he agreed to do *by virtue of the authority of the warrant granted to him by England for African Lodge.* In the same year Prince Hall gave authority to a number of coloured Masons in Providence, Rhode Island, to form a lodge there. For these actions he had no authority. The warrant for African Lodge which he had received from England was like any other English warrant of that, or the present, time. It permitted the holders to establish a lodge, make Masons, and elect successive Masters of the lodge. It also enjoined the holders to obey the *Constitutions* of the Grand Lodge of England and to keep in regular contact with the Grand Lodge. Later apologists for Prince Hall's actions claim that he was issued with a patent by the Grand Master of England in 1791 appointing him a Provincial Grand Master in North America. There is no record of such a patent in the *Register of Patents and Warrants* and the two typescript versions of it that have been published are so full of anachronisms as to be obvious forgeries to any competent Masonic historian.

Prince Hall died in 1808, but the African Lodge continued. They attempted to make new contact with England in 1824. The petitioners appear to have been totally unaware that African Lodge had been removed from the register and that a union had taken place in England. As the Grand Lodge of Massachusetts had been in existence for a considerable period there was no possibility of the United Grand Lodge of England renewing or issuing a new warrant for a lodge within Massachussets. In 1827 the African Lodge declared itself independent of any Grand Lodge as the African Grand Lodge No. 1 claiming full rights to charter subordinate lodges. In 1815 similar steps had been taken by the coloured lodge in Philadelphia and in the 1820s a self-constituted coloured lodge appeared in New York. In 1848 representatives of various coloured lodges came together in Boston to form a National Grand Lodge. This in turn began to set up a series of State Grand Lodges but, as happened in other Grand Lodges, harmony was turned to discord and many groups withdrew and formed state-based Prince Hall Grand Lodges.

Freemasonry flourished amongst coloured men and once Grand Lodges became established the various additional degrees and orders were adopted and a great deal of charitable work was carried out. Prince Hall Freemasonry has spread from the United States to Canada and the islands of the Caribbean and West Indies, where separate Grand Lodges have evolved. Since 1867 there has been a Prince Hall Grand Lodge in Liberia.

167
A Japanese lacquer and mother-of-pearl box, c.1870, made for the Masonic market.

The Masonic history of Central and South America is very complex. It has been made more so by the existence in the early nineteenth century in Spain, Portugal, and South America of an organization called the Loggia Lautaro. Masquerading as a Masonic organization, it was in fact a network of cells of political revolutionaries seeking democracy in the Iberian Peninsula and freedom from Spain and Portugal for their Central and South American colonies. As with the American and French Revolutions, it has been falsely claimed that the various South American revolutionary movements were masonically based and led by Freemasons.

Throughout the nineteenth century Grand Lodges and Grand Orients proliferated in Central and South America. In each of the countries there is a recognized Masonic authority and in many there are, or have been, irregular bodies. For the most part the irregular bodies have been declared so because they have broken one of the fundamental rules of Freemasonry by involving themselves *as Freemasons* in politics and religion. British Freemasonry was introduced into South America in the nineteenth century, but by far the greatest influence was the European Grand Orient style of Freemasonry. The result, when combined with influences from North America, has produced an amalgam of simplicity and drama fitting the volatile personalities of South America.

Regular Freemasonry now exists throughout the free world. Having come initially from the British Isles it has developed and acquired local idiosyncrasies but has remained true to the original principles and tenets.

168
Viscount Hayashi, Ambassador of Japan to Great Britain. Initiated in Empire Lodge No. 2108, London, he is wearing the regalia of a Past Senior Grand Warden of England, 1904.

169
King Oscar II of Sweden. Grand Master of Swedish Freemasonry and appointed a Past Grand Master of England, 1888.

One of the greatest delights for a Freemason who travels is to be able to experience the wide variety of means by which these principles and tenets are handed on, to experience the similarities and the differences but still to recognize a common core. Freemasonry is truly a worldwide brotherhood in the proper sense of that phrase. To call Freemasonry worldwide or international is not, as the conspiracy theorists would have us believe, to imply an international organization with a central controlling body. Each Grand Lodge, or Grand Orient, is a fiercely independent, sovereign, self-governing body owing allegiance to no other. Any attempts to form supra-national bodies have always fallen down because they would have involved a loss of sovereignty on the part of the participating Grand Lodges. In North America there are various annual conferences at which leaders of the Grand Lodges meet to discuss common problems. *Discuss* is the operative word, for any recommendations the conference arrive at have no force unless they are debated and accepted by the individual Grand Lodges. The strength of Freemasonry has been the simplicity and commonality of its principles and tenets combined with the ability to adapt the means of passing on those principles and tenets via the widely disparate national and cultural characteristics of those who have embraced Freemasonry. Any attempt to impose a supra-national governing body on Freemasonry would inevitably lead to attempts at standardization and a consequent loss of the diversity that has enriched Freemasonry.

What links Freemasonry throughout the world is not a desire for central control or dominance but a belief that, regardless of race, religion, politics, or class, there are basic ideals that unite mankind; that, if put into practice on a wide scale, can only enrich the world; and, in the words of the first of the Ancient Charges, be 'the means of conciliating true friendship among persons that [otherwise] must have remained at a perpetual distance'.

170 Below
Crown Prince Frederick of the Netherlands, 1797-1881, in his regalia as Grand Master. He presented the Grand East of the Netherlands with their present Hall.

171 Below right
Certificate issued by the Grand Lodge of Hungary. Freemasonry was banned in Hungary in 1920.

Epilogue: The Struggle for Truth

AND SO our tale is told; our story of the Craft is at an end. But what of the future? Will this 'peculiar system of morality' that has survived as we see it today for over 250 years continue to thrive for three centuries more? It has contrived to flourish in the face of hostility and active persecution throughout the course of its history and is now firmly established across every continent—absent only where democracy is absent and where unreason prevails.

But its hold is only as strong—or as fragile—as that of democracy itself, and where Freemasonry is threatened it is a clear sign that democratic structures are themselves under threat. This is not, however, always immediately apparent. Attacks upon the Craft in North America, for example, have been religious rather than political—based upon the false assumption that Freemasonry is a religion—and have centred on the claim that it is inimical to Christianity and the Christian Church, to the extent even of being an agent of Satan! Such misapprehensions can be countered only by a resolute determination on the part of Freemasons themselves to refute, patiently and without acrimony, every condemnatory statement and false accusation against the Craft and to ensure that the propagators of anti-Masonic lies are exposed.

In England, alas, anti-Masonry is at once more subtle and more firmly entrenched, for the Craft is under constant assault not only from religious bigots but also from unthinking populists of both the extreme left and extreme right of British politics. These attacks are fuelled by books such as the late Stephen Knight's *The Brotherhood* and Martin Short's more recent and immeasurably more venomous attack, *Inside the Brotherhood*. Both of these works—allegedly 'researched' in depth—abound in mistakes, distortions, illogical arguments, and the repetition of old and long exposed fables and lies, and yet they have been publicized and promoted by press and television alike as sound and scholarly productions that reflect a true state of affairs.

Political hostility towards the Craft is exemplified by politicians who lose no opportunity to lay baseless charges of corruption at Freemasonry's door. And then there is religious bigotry, as prevalent in Britain as in the USA. Ignorant and fanatic fundamentalists wage a ceaseless campaign of hatred against the Craft, seizing upon every disturbed ex-Mason as a witness to the supposed Satanic nature of Freemasonry. Freemasonry is not, and can never be, either a religion or a substitute for religion. But the fundamentalist refuses to face the truth, just as he refuses to face up to the psychological inadequacy that lies behind his hysterical attacks upon a body of men who have never, in the entire course of their history, persecuted or unjustly condemned anyone, whether for their religious beliefs or for any other reason.

In the past it has been the practice of Freemasonry to ignore public attacks made upon it, relying instead on the common sense of the public to see how unjust were the fantasies and twisted arguments of the anti-Masons. But now, because Freemasons are denied the right of reasoned reply in the media, the Craft must publicize itself to present a true image to a public familiar only with the false mask.

Thus after decades of seeking to maintain its privacy—as it had every right to do—Freemasonry has now become more open, reserving to itself as 'secrets' only its traditional modes of recognition as used within the confines of the lodge. No longer can opponents claim that the Craft is a 'secret society', hiding itself from public view. There never was anything to hide; but anti-Masons would still have the public believe otherwise. They are now unable to make spurious capital from the 'penalty clauses' of the Obligations in the Craft degree ceremonies, or from the Sacred Word in the ceremonies of the Holy Royal Arch (the removal of which was not, incidentally, in response to outside pressure but in deference to the wishes of the many Masons who had pointed out the anachronism of both 'penalty clauses' and Word and their liability to wilful misconstruction on the part of Freemasonry's enemies). Instead, the anti-Masons have turned their attention to the so-called Additional Degrees, seeking some sinister meaning and malevolent controlling junta within them—to the bewilderment of those Masons who are members of such degrees and who *know* that there is nothing whatsoever within them incompatible with a man's civil, moral, or religious duties, nor anything inimical to the Christian or any other faith.

This internal certainty is, sadly, no longer enough. Freemasons themselves must demonstrate by their own words and deeds that the Craft

172-3 **Opposite**
Freemasonry flourished even in times of war, many men risking their lives in Prisoner of War camps to continue their Masonry. These plates show French POW jewels; aprons used at Mafeking, the First World War and in occupied Jersey; officers' jewels from scrap metal on the Burma railroad; a ritual passed through camps in Germany; and a Bible used in Singapore.

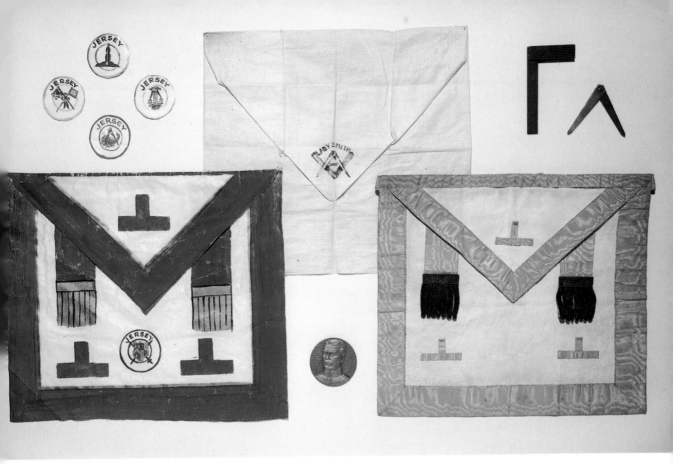

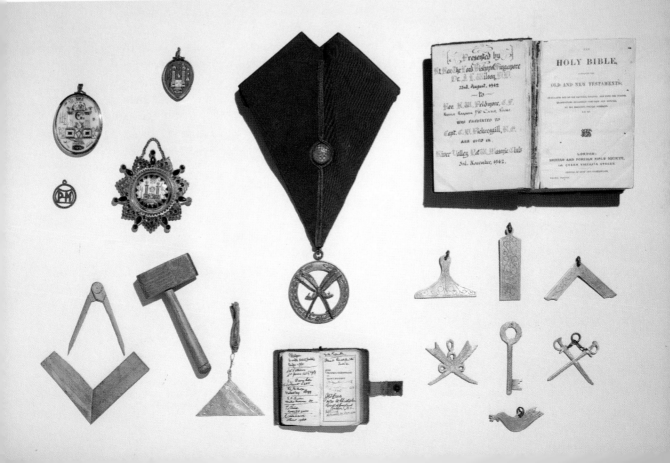

is a movement dedicated to the principles of freedom, tolerance, and brotherly love. It is indeed a carefully structured and close-knit organization, but its structure is wholly democratic, not autocratic, and it possesses no secret, inner cabal controlling its members.

Possessing no secrets in the ordinary meaning of the word, Freemasonry has no need of secrecy. Its members are proud to be Freemasons and have no desire to hide the fact of their membership from the world at large. The Craft itself can and will face its opponents with no weapons other than honesty and truth. It will rebut lies with truth, oppose hatred with tolerance, and endure mockery with resignation; it has no need to emulate the moral turpitude of its opponents, for it knows that it is guilty of no crime and of no sin. Secure in this knowledge it will advance as it always has done the cause of justice and of peace. It can do no other, for this is the very purpose of its being.

Bibliography

1 There are many Lodges of Research throughout the world, the majority of which produce *Transactions*. The principal is the Quatuor Coronati Lodge No. 2076, London, whose *Transactions, Ars Quatuor Coronatorum*, are a storehouse of Masonic history.

2 The governing bodies of the various Masonic Orders throughout the world publish official proceedings, yearbooks, constitutions and regulations, and, in many cases, official histories. Similarly many lodges, and their equivalents in the other Masonic Orders, produce histories—usually as private publications for circulation among the members.

3. The bibliography of Freemasonry is enormous. In 1910–11 Wolfstieg published his *Bibliographie der Freimaurerischen Literatur* in 3 volumes listing over 50,000 volumes. The readers of this book might find the following volumes of use in pursuing some of the themes the present authors have outlined.

Baynard, S.W., *History of the Supreme Council 33 Degree of the Northern Jurisdiction of the USA* (Boston, 1938).

Benimelli, Jose A.F., *Los Archivos Secretos Vaticanos y la Masoneria* (Caracas, 1976).

Benimelli, Jose A.F., *El Contubernio Judeo-masonico-comunista* (Madrid, 1982).

Benimelli, Jose A.F., *La Masoneria despuès del Concilio* (Barcelona, 1977).

Benimelli, Jose A.F., *Masoneria Española Contemporanea*. Vol. I 1800–1868. *Hasta Nuestros Dias*; Vol. II 1869 (Madrid, 1980).

Benimelli, Jose A.F., *Masoneria, Iglesia e Illustraciòn*, 4 vols (Madrid, 1976–7).

Butterfield, Paul H., *Centenary. The First Hundred Years of English Freemasonry in the Transvaal 1878–1978* (Johannesburg, 1978).

Carr, Harry, *The Early French Exposures* (London, 1971).

Carr, Harry, *The Freemason at Work*, rev. edn. (London, 1983).

Carr, Harry, *Harry Carr's World of Freemasonry* (London, 1984).

Chevallier, Pierre, *Histoire de la Franc-Maçonnerie Française*, 3 vols. (Paris, 1974–5).

Coil, Henry W., *Masonic Encyclopaedia* (New York, 1961).

Coil, Henry W. and Sherman, John D., *A Documentary History of Prince Hall and Other Black Fraternal Orders* (Missouri Lodge of Research, 1982).

Collaveri, François, *La Franc Maçonnerie des Bonaparte* (Paris, 1982).

Collected Prestonian Lectures, The, Vol. I 1925–60; Vol. II 1961–74; Vol. III 1975–86 (London, 1965–88).

Cook, C.W., *Colonial Freemasonry (USA)* (Missouri Lodge of Research, 1974).

Cooper, A.A., *The Freemasons of South Africa* (Cape Town, 1986).

Cotte, Roger, *La Musique Maçonnique et ses Musiciens* (Braine-le-Comte, 1975).

Crossle, Philip, *Irish Masonic Records* (Dublin, 1973).

Denslow, Ray, *10,000 Famous Freemasons* (Richmond, VA, n.d.)

Denslow, Ray, *A History of Royal Arch Masonry*, 3 vols. (N.p.p. (USA), 1956).

Di Bernardo, Giuliano, *Freemasonry and its Image of Man. A Philosophical investigation* (Tunbridge Wells, 1989).

Dumenil, Lynn, *Freemasonry and American Culture 1880–1930* (Princeton University Press, 1984).

Draffen, George, *Scottish Masonic Records 1736–1950* (Edinburgh, 1951).

Dyer, Colin, *Symbolism in Craft Freemasonry* (London, 1976).

Dyer, colin, *The Grand Stewards and their Lodge* (London, 1985).

Dyer, Colin, *William Preston and His Work* (London, 1987).

Gould, R.F., *History and Antiquities of Freemasonry*, 3 vols. (London, 1982–87).

Gould, R.F., *History and Antiquities of Freemasonry*, revised by H. Poole, 4 vols. (London, 1951).

Gould, R.F., *Military Lodges 1723–1889* (London, 1899).

Grantham, J.A., *An Introduction to Mark Masonry*, 2nd edn. (Buxton, 1935).

Grantham, J.A., *History of the Grand Lodge of Mark Master Masons* (London, 1960).

Haffner, Christopher, *The Craft in the East* (Hong Kong, 1977).

Haffner, Christopher, *Workman Unashamed. The testimony of a Christian Freemason* (London, 1989).

Hamill, John, *The Craft. A History of English Freemasonry* (Wellingborough, 1986).

Harris, Ray B., *History of the Supreme Council 33rd Degree . . . of the Southern Jurisdiction of the USA*, 3 vols. (Washington DC, 1964–71).

Hass, Ludwik, *Wolnomulartwo w Europie Snodkowo-Wschodniej w XVIII i XIX wieku* (Wroclaw, 1982).

Henderson, Kent, *Masonic World Guide*, 2nd edn. (London, 1989).

Henderson, Kent, *The Masonic Grand Masters of Australia* (Melbourne, 1988).

Holtorf, Jurgen, *Die Verschwiegene Bruderschaft, Freimaurer-Logen: Legende und Wirklichkeit* (Munich, 1983).

Horne, Alec, *King Solomon's Temple in the Masonic Tradition* (Wellingborough, 1972).

Horne, Alec, *The York Legend in the Old Charges* (London, 1978).

Hughan, W.J., *Origins of the English Rite of Freemasonry*, 3rd edn. (Leicester, 1925).

Hutchinson, William, *The Spirit of Freemasonry*, 1775, reprint, with an introduction by Trevor Stewart (Wellingborough, 1987).

Jackson, A.C.F., *Rose Croix, A History of the Ancient and Accepted Rite for England*, 2nd edn. (London, 1987).

Jackson, Keith, *Beyond the Craft* (London, 1980).

Johnson, Melvin M., *The Beginning of Freemasonry in America* (New York, 1924).

Jones, Bernard, *Freemasons' Guide and Compendium*, 2nd edn. (London, 1956).

Jones, Bernard, *Freemasons' Book of the Royal Arch*, 2nd edn. revised by Harry Carr and A.R. Hewitt (London, 1969).

Keuss, Gustav and Scheichelbauer, Bernhard, *200 Jahre Freimauerei in Osterreich* (Vienna, 1976).

Knoop, D. and Jones, G.P., *An Introduction to Freemasonry* (Manchester, 1937).

Knoop, D. and Jones, G.P., *The Genesis of Freemasonry*, reprint (London, 1978).

Knoop, D. and Jones, G.P., *Handlist of Masonic Documents*, 3rd edn. (Manchester, 1967).

Knoop, D. and Jones, G.P., The Medieval Mason, 3rd rev edn. (Manchester, 1967).

Knoop, D. and Jones, G.P., *The Scottish Mason and the Mason Word* (Manchester, 1939).

Knoop, D., Jones, G.P. and Hamer, D., *Early Masonic Catechisms*, 2nd edn. (London, 1975).

Knoop, D., Jones, G.P. and Hamer, D., *Early Masonic Pamphlets*, reprint (London, 1978).

Lamonby, W.F., *Some Notes on Freemasonry in Australasia from the Earliest Times to the Present Day* (London, 1906).

Lane, John, *Masonic Records 1717–1895*, 2nd edn. (London, 1895).

Lenhoff, Eugen, *The Freemasons*, translated by Einar Frame, 1936, reprint (London, 1978).

Lenhoff, Eugen and Posner, Oskar, *Internationales Freimaurerlexicon* (Zurich, 1932).

Lepper, J.H., Crossle, P. and Parkinson, R.E., *History of the Grand Lodge of Ireland*, 2 vols (Dublin, 1925–57).

Mackey, Albert G., *Encyclopaedia of Freemasonry*, various edns.

MacNulty, W. Kirk, *The Way of the Craftsman. A Search for the Spiritual Essence of Freemasonry* (London, 1988).

McKenzie, K.R.H., *The Royal Masonic Cyclopaedia*, 1877, reprint with an introduction by John Hamill and R.A. Gilbert (Wellingborough, 1987).

Mellor, Alec, *Dictionaire de la Franc-Maçonnerie et des Franc-Maçons* (Paris, 1971).

Mellor, Alec, *Histoire des Scandales Maçonniques* (Paris, 1982).

Mellor, Alec, *Our Separated Brethren the Freemasons* (London, 1971).

Naudon, Paul, *Histoire générale de la Franc-Maçonnerie* (Fribourg, 1981).

Oliver, George, *The Book of the Lodge*, 3rd edn. 1864. Introduced by R.S.E. Sandbach (Wellingborough, 1986).

Pace, M de, *Introducing Freemasonry* (London, 1983).

Partner, Peter, *The Murdered Magicians: The Templars and Their Myths* (Wellingborough, 1987).

Pick, F.L. and Knight, G.N., *Freemasons Pocket Reference Book*, 3rd edn. revised by F.H. Smyth (London, 1983).

Pick, F.L. and Knight, G.N., *Pocket History of Freemasonry*, 7th edn. (London, 1983).

Prestige, H.H.C., *A Century of the Allied Masonic Degrees* (London, 1976).

Preston, William, *Illustrations of Masonry*, 11th edn. 1801, with an introduction by Colin Dyer (Wellingborough, 1985).

Ritus in Tempelbouw, *De beoefening der Koninklijke Kunst in Nederland* (The Hague, 1971).

Roberts, Allen E., *The Craft and its Symbols* (Richmond, VA, 1974).

Roberts, Allen E., *House Undivided. The Story of Freemasonry and the Civil War* (Missouri Lodge of Research, 1961).

Roberts, Allen E., *Masonry under Two Flags* (Washington DC, 1968).

Roberts, J.M., *The Mythology of the Secret Societies* (London, 1972).

Robertson, J. Roass, *The History of Freemasonry in Canada from its Introduction in 1749*, 2 vols (Toronto, 1899).

Sadler, Henry, *Masonic Facts and Fictions*, reprint with an introduction by John Hamill (Wellingborough, 1985).

Sandbach, R.S.E., *Priest and Freemason. The Life of George Oliver* (Wellingborough, 1988).

Stevenson, David, *The First Freemasons. Scotland's Early Lodges and their Members* (Aberdeen, 1988).

Stevenson, David, *The Origins of Freemasonry. Scotland's Century 1590–1710* (Cambridge, 1988).

Stubbs, Sir James, *Freemasonry in My Life* (London, 1985).

Tatsch, J. Hugo, *Freemasonry in the Thirteen Colonies* (New York, 1929).

Thory, C.A., *Acta Latomorum, ou Chronologie de l'Histoire de la Franche-Maçonnerie, Française, et Étrangère*, 2 vols (Paris, 1815).

United Grand Lodge of England, *Grand Lodge 1717–1967* (London, 1967).

Vaughan, William P., *The Anti-Masonic Party in the United States 1826–1843* (University Press of Kentucky, 1983).

Voorhis, Harold V.B., *Masonic Organisations and Allied Orders and Degrees. A Cyclopaedic Handbook* (Npp, 1952).

Voorhis, Harold V.B., *Negro Masonry in the USA* (New York, 1940).

Waite, A.E., *A New Cyclopaedia of Freemasonry*, 2nd edn., 2 vols (London 1921).

Waite, A.E., *The Secret Tradition in Freemasonry*, 2 vols (London, 1911).

Walkes, Joseph A., *Black Square and Compasses* (Npp, 1979).

Wells, Roy A., *Freemasonry in London from 1785* (London, 1984).

Wells Roy A., *Royal Arch Matters* (London, 1984).

Wells, Roy A., *The Rise and Development of Organised Freemasonry* (London, 1986).

Yarker, John, *The Arcane Schools* (Belfast, 1909).

Yates, Frances A., *The Rosicrucian Enlightenment* (London, 1972).

Index of Personal Names